Elgg Social Networking

Create and manage your own social network site using this free open-source tool

Mayank Sharma

PUBLISHING

BIRMINGHAM - MUMBAI

Elgg Social Networking

First published: March 2008

Production Reference: 1190308

Published by Packt Publishing Ltd.
32 Lincoln Road
Olton
Birmingham, B27 6PA, UK.

ISBN 978-1-847192-80-6

www.packtpub.com

Cover Image by Vinayak Chittar (vinayak.chittar@gmail.com)

Credits

Author

Mayank Sharma

Reviewer

Diego Ramirez

Senior Acquisition Editor

David Barnes

Development Editor

Rashmi Phadnis

Technical Editor

Ajay Shanker

Editorial Team Leader

Mithil Kulkarni

Project Manager

Patricia Weir

Project Coordinator

Patricia Weir

Indexer

Monica Ajmera

Proofreader

Nina Hasso

Production Coordinator

Aparna Bhagat

Cover Designer

Aparna Bhagat

About the Author

Author name followed by his details. This information needs to be provided by the Development Editor.

Mayank Sharma is a contributing editor at SourceForge, Inc's Linux.com. He also writes a monthly column for Packt Publishing. Mayank has contributed several technical articles to the IBM developerWorks where he hosts a Linux Security blog. When not writing, he teaches courses on Open Source topics at the Indian Institute of Technology, Delhi, as guest lecturer.

Thanks to my mom Shashi and dad Rakesh for laying down tough standards, and younger brother Shashank who beat me at book-writing to become my mentor.

Gratitude to David Barnes for guiding me from start to finish, to Rashmi Phadnis for her edits, to Patricia Weir for managing and scheduling the book, and to the Elgg developers and community for such a wonderful project.

About the Reviewer

Diego Ramírez is a computer scientist from the Los Andes University in Colombia, and is currently working at Somos más, a Colombian non-profit that is involved in the development of methodologies and tools to aid the articulation of non-profits.

He has a rich experience in building Web applications for the corporate as well as non-profit sectors in Colombia. Between them, are the open source movement, data mining over social network data, and figuring out how the information and communication technologies could be used to empower people to make a difference in the world.

I want to say thanks to all of the Elgg team! Working with them has been very constructive, and has given me even more reason to believe in the open source model. Things can be afforded through sharing of knowledge and experience without any limitations.

In memory of my grandfather H. C. Sharma and grandmother Shyma Sharma.

Table of Contents

Preface

Elgg is an open-source social web application licensed under GPL version 2, and runs on the LAMP (Linux, Apache, MySQL, and PHP) or WAMP (Windows, Apache, MySQL, PHP) platform. It offers a networking platform, combining elements of blogging, e-portfolios, news feed aggregation, file sharing, and social networking. Elgg has its own plug-in architecture, and can use plug-ins to provide a calendar and a wiki. It supports a number of open standards including RSS, LDAP for authentication, FOAF, and XML-RPC for integration with most third-party blogging clients. It can be integrated with MediaWiki, Moodle, Drupal, and WebCT.

Elgg provides each user with a personal weblog, file repository (with podcasting capabilities), an online profile, and an RSS reader. Additionally, all of a user's content can be tagged with keywords—so they can connect with other users with similar interests and create their own personal learning network. However, where Elgg differs from a regular weblog or a commercial social network (such as MySpace) is the degree of control each user is given over who can access their content. Each profile item, blog post, or uploaded file can be assigned its own access restrictions—from fully public to readable only by a particular group or individual.

Using Elgg is the easiest way to create your own fully customized, hosted social network for your business, organization, or group of friends. Elgg communities can include blogs, discussion groups, media galleries, friends' lists, and much more. Because it's open source, and has many plug-ins, Elgg can be extended in unlimited ways. Elgg lets you host your own Facebook-style social network and retain complete control over how it works. This book shows you all you need to know to create safe, fun social networks.

While anybody can use Elgg to create their social network, it is especially useful in education as it has many features making it suitable for e-learning, including groups, communities, and blogs that can be used for online classes where students can communicate in a new way with each other and with students around the world—in a managed, protected environment, creating what its authors term a "personal learning landscape".

What This Book Covers

Chapter 1 covers the basics of social networking, runs over some popular social networks and goes through some of the features that are essential to online social networking. It introduces Elgg, and highlights some of the benefits of deploying one's own social network.

In Chapter 2 we use publicly accessible Elgg-installations like Ubuntero.org, the upcoming network of Ubuntu users, developers, and fans and the Elgg.org website itself as examples, to see the screens and options first-hand. After reading through the chapter, you should have a fairly good idea of what your very own Elgg-based social network will be able to do.

Chapter 3 deals with the users. We discuss several ways of inviting users to join the network, some of which can be used by ordinary users, while others are only for administrators. You'll learn to connect with other users on the network. We also run through Elgg's built-in mechanisms for attracting visitors to join the network. In between, we cover various account settings that a user can alter. After reading this chapter, you should have no trouble adding, managing or connecting to members in your Elgg network.

Chapter 4 covers one of the most exciting features — blogs. It will help you deal with abusive and off-topic content. You will learn to share video files, PDFs, images, and podcasts.

Chapter 5 Social networking is all about communities. This chapter will teach you to create communities, manage them, and manage the content in communities.

Chapter 6 You don't want your site to look like any other. It should have a unique style of its own. What better way to make this happen than using theming engines? This chapter will teach you all about themes. By the time you are through with this chapter, you will be able to create a unique theme for your site.

Chapter 7 covers some of the important Elgg plug-ins that'll give you better control in administering your site.

Appendix A deals with installing Elgg in the popular LAMP web application environment of Linux, Apache, MySQL, and PHP. Since Apache, MySQL, and PHP can also run under a Windows operating system, you can also set up Elgg to serve your purpose in a "WAMP" environment, and this appendix covers this too.

Appendix B is a list of case studies that will help you relate to popular real-world networking sites that use Elgg.

Who is This Book for

This book is aimed at people interested in social networking and e-learning teachers.

Conventions

In this book, you will find a number of styles of text that distinguish between different kinds of information. Here are some examples of these styles, and an explanation of their meaning.

There are three styles of code. Code words in text are shown as follows: "We can include other contexts through the use of the `include` directive."

A block of code will be set as follows:

```
<object width="425" height="350"><param name="movie" value="http://
www.youtube.com/v/EgrfmSm0NWs"></param><param name="wmode"
value="transparent"></param><embed src="http://www.youtube.com/v/
EgrfmSm0NWs" type="application/x-
```

New terms and **important words** are introduced in a bold-type font. Words that you see on the screen, in menus or dialog boxes for example, appear in our text like this: "clicking the **Next** button moves you to the next screen".

Important notes appear in a box like this.

Tips and tricks appear like this.

Reader Feedback

Feedback from our readers is always welcome. Let us know what you think about this book, what you liked or may have disliked. Reader feedback is important for us to develop titles that you really get the most out of.

To send us general feedback, simply drop an email to `feedback@packtpub.com`, making sure to mention the book title in the subject of your message.

If there is a book that you need and would like to see us publish, please send us a note in the **SUGGEST A TITLE** form on www.packtpub.com or email suggest@packtpub.com.

If there is a topic that you have expertise in and you are interested in either writing or contributing to a book, see our author guide on www.packtpub.com/authors.

Customer Support

Now that you are the proud owner of a Packt book, we have a number of things to help you to get the most from your purchase.

Errata

Although we have taken every care to ensure the accuracy of our content, mistakes do happen. If you find a mistake in one of our books—maybe a mistake in text or code—we would be grateful if you would report this to us. By doing this you can save other readers from frustration, and help to improve subsequent versions of this book. If you find any errata, report them by visiting http://www.packtpub.com/support, selecting your book, clicking on the **Submit Errata** link, and entering the details of your errata. Once your errata are verified, your submission will be accepted and the errata added to the list of existing errata. The existing errata can be viewed by selecting your title from http://www.packtpub.com/support.

Questions

You can contact us at questions@packtpub.com if you are having a problem with some aspect of the book, and we will do our best to address it.

1
Social Networks and Elgg

J. A. Barnes, in 1954, coined the term Social Network to refer to a map of the relationships between individuals, indicating the ways in which they are connected through various social familiarities ranging from casual acquaintance to close familial bonds.

Little did Barnes know that, five decades later, social networks, with the Internet as catalyst, would change the dynamics of interaction. Social networking on the Web has dissolved boundaries around the traditional physical networks.

There's no dearth of social networks on the Internet. This book is about using the Elgg social networking platform to create, run, and manage your own social network. To understand why you'd want to do this as against to using one of the publicly accessible networks, you have to understand what these networks are good for, and what their weak points are.

The idea behind a social networking website is simple — to 'hook up' people with similar interests. It works pretty much like a physical social network. You meet people, establish connections, keep up with the contacts, and continue the relationship. In a professional setting, many connections are established by intermediaries. These are people common to both parties involved, and facilitate initial contact. But there's a limit to physical social networks that you can be a part of.

This is where social networking over the Internet is so revolutionary. It allows you find like-minded people, beyond your physical network, and across timezones. You can simultaneously be part of an unimaginable number of social networks formed around fairly common topics like bands or a particular celebrity, to some obscure topics like a specific kind of hairdo or an element in the periodic table.

And you don't have to spend an awful lot of time looking for simpatico people. Online social networks allow you to search a network using particular key terms.

The best thing about social networking on the Web, is that it has been evolving with the times. As they grow, the pervasive social networks offer new opportunities for everyone — from school going teenagers to multinational corporations.

Types of Social Networks

So you all know what social networking on the Web is, and have probably used at least a couple of these services to keep in touch with friends and ex-colleagues. But before you get down to building your social network, spend some time analyzing the purpose, intent, and the audience makeup of these social networks. Once you understand these, you'll be able to customize your network, accordingly.

In very simple terms, there are two kinds of social networks:

1. *The indifferent social network*: These are the ones you've all probably used. MySpace, Facebook, Orkut are all examples of the indifferent social network. These networks have no bias, or prejudice, against their users. Whether you are joining to reconnect with old friends or to make new ones, you are welcome all the same. They don't give preferential treatment to users of a particular profession and are, in fact, totally disinterested in what you do. You get the idea! I am sure you are on one such network and so are your peers.

2. *The niche network*: On the other hand, you have discreet networks like Within3 [https://www.within3.com/]. Within3 is a community of physicians and health researchers. As per its website, Within3 also helps members recruit patients for clinical trials, and keep them informed of the latest medical advancements. Registration on the website is by invitation only, and is open for physicians or researchers in the health sciences, or for students training for an advanced health science degree. But registration-by-invite isn't the distinguishing feature of a discreet network. It's their scope, which is big enough for the members, but limited for a general audience. An

example of this is U.S. Presidential candidate Barack Obama's social network MyBarackObama [http://my.barackobama.com/]. Anyone can register on this network, but you wouldn't find many Republicans there, now would you?

This book will help you build your own niche social network. Niche doesn't necessarily mean small. Dedicated networks can have as many members as publicly accessible social networks. The idea of running your own social network isn't to give MySpace or Facebook a run for their money. A customized social network is a virtual manifestation of scratching a common itch.

How Can a Social Network Help You?

So, you understand why you want to run a social network. Or do you? How can running a social network help you? Why should you go through the pain of hosting, managing, and most importantly paying for your own social network, when you can join one for free? There are several reasons why you'd want to do this. I'll share the three most common ones:

1. *Bring your customers closer.* Getting to know your customer helps companies provide a better service. And what better place to interact with them than on the Internet. Just yesterday, I saw a local hair salon's advertisement, which flashed very proudly, "Join us on Orkut". But why use a third-party service when you can run your own. With Elgg, you can set up your own social network and integrate it with your existing website. The Swiss watch company, Swatch, "talks" to its customers via its Elgg-powered social network, Swatch The Club [http://www.swatchtheclub.com/].

2. *Dissolve physical boundaries.* Doing things on the Internet has the positive side effect of eradicating physical barriers. If you have to work with physically separated people that are connected through a strong common thread, like various colleges of a university, or regional offices of a multinational corporation, a social network is an ideal extension of a bulletin board or a company intranet. The University of Brighton has several campuses all over the UK. Thanks to their Elgg-powered network, Community@Brighton [`http://community.brighton.ac.uk/`], the students and teachers are all connected to each other. In Colombia, the Somos Más Non Government Organization is using Elgg-powered networks to bring the various NGOs working with children and the physically disabled, under one roof.

3. *Stay focused.* While getting in touch with your old friends is good, the whole idea of "going out" in an online social network is meeting like-minded people. You might not realize it, but the popular publicly accessible networks put a lot of effort into making sure you meet new and like-minded people. A social network, based around a common interest, is an extension of a fan site. So, if you are a fan of Johnny Cash, what better way to meet people who share your passion for country music than with a Johnny Cash social network site. Ubuntero [`http://ubuntero.org/`] is an Elgg-powered network for the developers and users of the popular open source Linux distribution, Ubuntu.

Can you identify yourself with any of these situations?

I bet you do. And that's what this book is about. It'll help you set up and manage your own social network on the Internet with Elgg. It doesn't take much effort, but the benefits are clearly visible. You get the option to customize and brand your social network as you want. This is also helpful if you want to integrate the social network into your existing website. Depending on your purpose, a public social network might be too big. There's nothing like creating a specialized and targeted one that keeps you in-charge.

Tools of the Trade

A social networking website is a Web 2.0 service. The term Web 2.0, coined by O'Reilly media in 2004, isn't a technology update to the Internet, but rather refers to the so-called second generation of web-based services that encourages reader-participation.

Two-way communication forms the basis for a read-write environment of a social network. A social network is a conglomeration of several internet communication tools and services. Let's take a look at some of them.

Blogs: A blog or a weblog is, literally, a "log" on the Web. A blog is a diary-style site, in which the author called the "blogger" writes content that is displayed in reverse chronological order. Technorati, a blog search engine, tracks more than 50 million blogs.

Blogs are an ideal platform for social networking. People use them to express themselves by commentating on news, or to keep in touch with friends and family. Blogs are typically a combination of text, images, and other multimedia content like audio and video. They can also link to other blogs or web pages. Blogs also allow, rather encourage, people to leave comments on individual entries, which bring in a sense of interaction.

Forums: Online forum boards allow members to post and discuss a particular topic. They facilitate the exchange of information between members. A forum is composed of several "threads". Discussions take place inside these threads in the form of member written posts.

Forum boards are an essential part of any social community. Generally, a forum board is sub-divided into several forums, each with their own discussions. For example, a software project might host a forum, sub-divided into a "user" and a "developer" forum.

Developer discussion :: Forum		
🔊	View as Blog		
Discussion Topic	**Started by**	**Comments**
How to restrict people in the same community delete the file in storage?	mic	0
Please help with the Vietnamese language file	mic	4
bug in messages plugin?	cmcompto	2
Strings in Theme Keyword Args	jP Loh	0
loggedinusers plugin returning error	cmcompto	6
Levels of acces restrictions for personal data	Bahne Carstensen	8
Profile commenting plugin not working	devin calloway	6

Communities: A social network wouldn't be complete without a community. Forming communities can be called the crux of social networking. By allowing members to create and control their own communities, social networking sites help people pin-point like-minded peers.

In another sense, a virtual community can also form around forum boards. Regular members develop a sense of responsibility and ownership around their forum. By contributing and helping others, they encourage interaction and exchange of information between users.

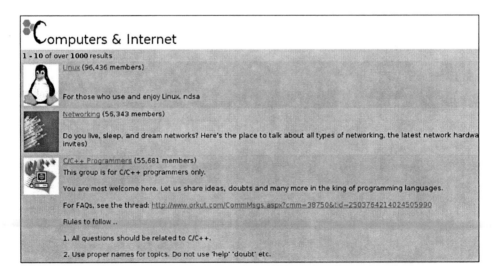

There are certain elements, without which social networking on the Web wouldn't be possible, despite all the tools explained above.

Profiles: Almost all social networking websites require members to create an account. Depending on the kind of social networking website you're registering at, this process can be quite extensive. This is because along with creating an account, you are also asked to fill up certain details about yourself, which will be your online profile.

A profile can have work related information (education, work location, job title, work experience, and so on) or personal information (favorite movies, books, sports, and so on), or a mix of both. The more detailed and clear your profile, the better your chance of finding compatible people.

Anthony Bryan ①

Metalinker.org Content Distribution
Miami/Fort Lauderdale Area

Profile | Connections

Current	◆ Owner at **Metalinker.org**
Education	● Nova Southeastern University ● Palm Beach Atlantic University
Connections	✦ 22 connections
Industry	Information Technology and Services
Websites	● Metalinker.org
Public Profile	http://www.linkedin.com/in/anthonybryan

👍 Recommend this person

☐ Send email   Download vCard

Ads by Google

Travel Writers:
Re-sell your travel content online. Editors: shop for quality content.
www.itravelsyndicate.com

We need writers
Publish, be read, and get paid. Start writing instantly!
www.blogit.com/

📄 **Summary**

I develop the Metalink framework which offers high availability self healing (automatic error correction) downloads and is used for

✦ **Anthony's Connections (22)**

Kelly Bryan
Technical recruiter

Friends: The whole idea of social networks is to find like-minded people. Making friends is the foremost activity. If a web service doesn't allow you to add friends, it can't be categorized as a social network.

Sharing: This is another important aspect of social networking. Meeting new people, without sharing, wouldn't make much sense. You can share information, ideas, pictures, or documents. A social networking website should let members share with others.

Tags: These are keywords assigned to some piece of information. A tag can refer to a picture, an article, or a podcast. Tags should be clear enough to describe the item. They ease searching and categorization of items. In fact, tags are so popular that they've paved the way for Folksonomy or collaborative tagging. By transferring indexing control to users, Folksonomy websites incite people to share. A good example of this is the social bookmarking website, Del.icio.us. In the context of a social network, tags are what connect people.

Feed syndication: A 'feed' on the Web refers to a data format that is used for serving frequently updated content. Content distributors make available a web feed which users can subscribe to. Web feeds have given birth to a special type of software called a feed aggregator. The good thing about feeds is that instead of personally keeping track of content changes, users leave the task to an aggregator, which can alert them as and when new content is generated. In the context of social networking, feeds of blogs, forums, or a community ensure members can keep track of the changes.

What's so Special About Elgg?

In this book, we'll use Elgg to deploy our social network. In March 2004, Ben Werdmuller and David Tosh, released Elgg as a platform for people to connect and share resources. A few years later, Elgg now powers social networks within several universities, educational institutes, and corporations, around the globe.

Elgg is Free and Open Source Software (FOSS), and is released under the GNU General Public License. It's free in terms of both price, and the freedom to modify its source code to improve or tweak it as per your requirements. It's based on the popular LAMP software bundle. LAMP is a culmination of the Linux operating system (OS), a prominent, UNIX-like, FOSS OS; the Apache web server, which as of March 2007 powers 58% of all websites on the Internet; MySQL database, used in over 10 million installations; and the PHP programming language, a powerful server-side scripting language.

Elgg allows you to create a social network and host it on your own infrastructure. You are free to modify its features to fit your specific needs. If you want, the developers also provide paid support and hosting around Elgg via their company called Curverider.

So, What can Elgg Do?

Elgg packs a lot of features that you'd want in your social network website. Using Elgg, members can have their own blogs, form and join communities, collect news and articles using feeds aggregation, and share files. Here's a full-feature list:

- Blogging
- File repositories for individuals and communities
- Podcast support
- Full access controls
- Supports tagging
- User profiles
- Full RSS support
- RSS aggregator
- Create communities
- Collaborative community blogs
- Create 'friends' networks
- Import content
- Publish to blog
- Thorough privacy controls
- Multilingual
- Branding/customization
- OpenID
- Import/export friends with FOAF.

Elgg can also be set up to integrate with other popular web-based tools like blogs and wikis. It can also be expanded with plug-ins to provide a calendar, a wiki, or advertisement.

Summary

In this first chapter, we've covered the basics of social networking. The idea behind the theoretical lesson on how people socialize on the Internet and the various types of social networking websites was to help you understand where your personalized network fits in the galaxy of social networking on the Web.

To set us up for the coming chapters, we've also been through some of the features that are essential to online social networking. I've introduced you to Elgg, listing all the features it supports, which are adequate to power a network of a dozen users or over 20,000. The next chapter will be a visual tour through Elgg.

2
A Tour around Elgg

Now that we have you believe that Elgg is a sprawling mansion, a tour of its facilities is in order. But, no! That analogy isn't accurate. Think of Elgg as a playground, or better-still, an under-construction theme park, and you are the architect. But before you can bring on the madness, let's understand the playground a little better.

Playing With Elgg-Powered Networks

To get a hang of how things are done in Elgg-land, we'll turn to a couple of Elgg-powered networks—the new and upcoming network of Ubuntu users and developers, Ubuntero.org; and Elgg's website itself, Elgg.org. As mentioned in Chapter 1, Elgg.org is run by the developers of Elgg, and is a test bed for all things Elgg as they roll off the assembly line.

Registering an account on Ubuntero.org and Elgg.org is free and open to anyone. I am using these free services because they'll closely resemble what your Elgg installation will look like, once we get to that point. Secondly, they're available on the Internet and accessible to anyone wanting to get a feel of Elgg. But remember, both are highly focused communites of Ubuntu and Elgg users and developers, and you shouldn't abuse that. I know you guys are a responsible bunch!

So without further ado, let's go register an account and get cracking.

Sign Up

Opening an account on Ubuntero.org is easy. Head over to the registration page (`http://ubuntero.org/_invite/register.php`) and simply enter your name and email address. Ubuntero.org will send you an email confirming your registration. The email has a link.

Ubuntero.org Administrator to me   show details 11:27 PM (2 m

Dear Mayank Sharma,

Thank you for registering with Ubuntero.org.

To join, visit the following URL:

   http://ubuntero.org/_invite/join.php?invitecode=i1j8owoi

Your email address has not been passed onto any third parties, and will be removed from our system within seven days.

Regards,

The Ubuntero.org team.

The link will fly you to a page that'll ask for the necessary details to complete the registration process. The page requests you to enter a username and a password. Once you've done that, click the **Join** button to complete the registration process. Users under thirteen years of age can't register on Ubuntero.

Join Ubuntero.org

Thank you for registering for an account with Ubuntero.org! Registration is completely free, but before you confirm your details, please take a moment to read the following documents:

- Ubuntero.org terms and conditions
- Privacy policy

Submitting the form below indicates acceptance of these terms. Please note that currently you must be at least 13 years of age to join the site.

Your name

Mayank Sharma

Your username - (Must be letters only)

geekybodhi

Enter a password

****

Your password again for verification purposes

****

☑ I am at least thirteen years of age.

Join

After you've entered all the information, Elgg will confirm that your account has been created with the username and password you selected. It also promises you that an email containing your username and password has been dispatched to your email address.

> Your account was created! You can now log in using the username and password you supplied. You have been sent an email containing these details for reference purposes.

Once you've logged on to the system, you'll be taken to the main index. But unlike your previous visits, you'll notice two changes—in the right-hand column and in the top bar. At the top of the page, there's a navigation bar with links to your blog, your file repository, your profile, and other items. The right-hand column carries information about you, your friends on the network, and your recent activity.

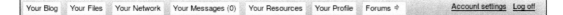

| Your Blog | Your Files | Your Network | Your Messages (0) | Your Resources | Your Profile | Forums ✦ | Account settings | Log off |

Account Settings

When you first log in to your Elgg account on Ubuntero.org, you should visit the **Account settings** link in the top right-corner of the page. From this page, you can change various aspects of your account like your email address and your name (if you are tired of your regular name!).

Mayank Sharma :: Edit user details

Edit user details | Your site picture | Change theme

Change your full name:

This name will be displayed throughout the system.

Your full name

Mayank Sharma

Your email address:

This will not be displayed to other users; you can choose to make an email address available via the profile screen.

Your email address

geekybodhi@gmail.com

Friendship moderation:

This allows you to choose who can list you as a friend.

Friendship moderation

No moderation: anyone can list you as a friend. (Recommended) ▾

Make comments public

Set this to 'yes' if you would like anyone to be able to comment on your resources (by default only logged-in users can). Note that this may make you vulnerable to spam.

Public comments:

○ Yes ● No

Typically, this should be the first link a new user, who has registered an account with an Elgg system, should click on. Apart from the basic pieces of identification information, the account settings page has some very interesting options as well. From this page, you can also change your password or render Ubuntero in one of the several languages it supports, including Italian, French, Spanish, Dutch, German, Swedish, Korean, and many more.

You can also choose to moderate all your friend requests. If you choose to do so, Elgg will send you an approval email whenever a user clicks to add you as a friend. If you'd like Elgg to send you email copies of the messages you receive on your Elgg inbox, you can do so from here. You can also change the page on which Elgg drops you upon login. For example, you can directly be taken to your blog, or the messages page after logging into Ubuntero. We'll discuss adding friends and the Elgg inbox, in forthcoming sections.

Your Profile

The user's profile is the most important part of social networking on the Web. It's your digital self, your online identity, expressed in certain preset parameters.

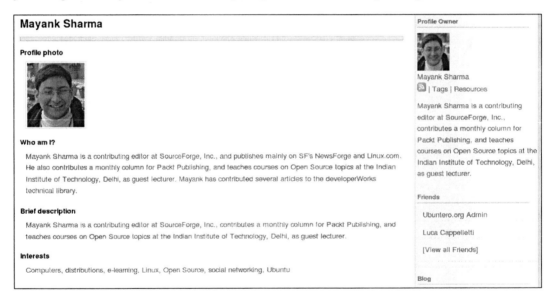

The profile page is the entrance door to your electronic portfolio. From the profile page, apart from editing the profile, you can also change your picture and manage widgets. We'll talk about widgets a little later.

Your profile tells others quite a bit about you. It's divided into sections to separate your basic details like your interests, likes, dislikes, and so on, from your physical location, your contact details, your level of education, and your employment status.

It's not mandatory to fill out all the details, but it's strongly recommended because it'll help Elgg find you people with similar interests. Oh yes! Did I mention that Elgg automatically creates links from your profile to others who share the same interests, likes, dislikes, and skills! Neat, huh?

Customize Your Account

You can, and should change the look and feel of your landscape. Some Elgg networks (like the now defunct Eduspaces.net) lets you choose from one of the ready made templates. If none matches your taste, you can let your imagination run wild by using Elgg's powerful templating design engine to create your own.

Select / Create / Edit Themes

Public Themes

The following are public themes that you can use to change the way your EduSpaces looks - these do not change the content only the appearance. Check the preview and then select the one you want. If you wish you can adapt one of these using the 'create theme' option below.

⦿	**Default Template**	Preview
○	**Differential**	Preview
○	**Light**	Preview
○	**Mandarin**	Preview
○	**Nonzero-blue**	Preview
○	**Nonzero-brown**	Preview
○	**Nonzero-green**	Preview
○	**Nonzero-magenta**	Preview
○	**Nonzero-red**	Preview
○	**TrulySimple**	Preview
○	**Default for Mac firefox**	Preview

Another important aspect of customizing the look and feel of your account is by re-arranging the widgets for your space. Ubuntero provides widgets that'll display or pull-in content from blogs, comment wall, files, profile, friends, video, and more.

Widget added.

Edit widget

Video widget

To embed videos from popular sites like Google Video and Youtube, obtain the embed HTML, paste it in the following form and configure your preferred size:

Video URL:	`<param name="movie" value="http://www.youtube.com/v/EDorTsCEdzk&rel=1" name="wmode" value="transparent"></param><embed src="http://www.youtube.com/v/EDorTsCEdzk&rel=1" type="application/x-shockwave-flash" wmode="transparent" width="425"`
Video size:	200 x 240

Access: Private ▾ Save widget

Define Access Privileges

Would you give out your contact information to complete strangers that you run into at the bookshop? Of course, not! Similarly, you wouldn't want everyone to know your phone number or the school you graduated from. In the physical world, a polite smile or refusal is your best form of protection!

Keeping the information safe online is a different matter, though. But with Elgg it's even more polite than the politest no! You can tell Elgg what part of your online self should be visible to visitors depending on whether they are logged on to the system or not.

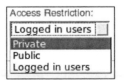

Access Restriction:
Logged in users
Private
Public
Logged in users

The default levels of access are "public", "logged in users", and "private". Public items are visible to anyone viewing your Elgg space. Relatively harmless information like your name, brief description, your job position, can be made "public". Information you want to share with other members logged into the system, relevant to the network, should be allowed to "logged in users" only. Information you don't want to share with anyone, should be kept as "private".

You can wrap these access restrictions around each and every profile item. Furthermore, these access privileges extend to anything you put up with Elgg, including your files, your blog posts, and so on.

Your Blog

Once you have your profile in place, it's time to share your thoughts through your blog. Apart from the actual text that goes into the blog entry, you need to take a couple of steps to make sure people read your blog. Organizing posts in categories helps keep things in order. Categorized information is also easily comprehended by visitors.

Add a new post

Post title:

Blogging with Elgg

Add External video

Post body:

B *I* <u>U</u> | ABC ≣ ≣ ≣ ≣ ≔ ≔ 🖼 ↺ ↻ ⚯ ✂ HTML ✌ ▾ ☺
🔍 🔍 ^A^B

Blogging with Elgg using the blog post editor is very simple. The blog editor resembles a basic text editor and features buttons to make text **bold,** *italics,* or <u>underlined</u>. You can also ~~strikethrough text~~, and even change paragraph alignment. That's me on the right.

Path: **div** »
img

The other powerful tool with Elgg blogs is keywords. Elgg's keywords facility assists in connecting to other resources and people. Keywords appear in a tag cloud, which are searchable. Use as many keywords as possible, but keep them relevant to the content in the post.

Elgg also lets you embed multimedia content like pictures and video clips from external sources into the post. You can also insert files from your repository into your post.

To help your readers connect to you, each blog post is accompanied by your photo, links to your profile, and keyword tags entered for that post.

Manage Your Files

Your Elgg account also lets you upload files. On Ubuntero, you can use this facility to upload your photos, assignments, coursework, etc up to a total of 1000 MB.

Mayank Sharma :: Files

Add a file or a folder | RSS feed for files

Root Folder

Subfolders

[Logged in users] Screenshots [Edit] [Delete]

Upload files and folders

Create a new folder

| To create a new folder, enter its name: | |
| Folder type: | Default file folder |

Of course, you can attach access privileges to all of these items to control who you want share them with. Once the items are in your repository, you can easily embed them into your weblog posts. You are also free to keep items private if you don't want anyone peeking at them.

The best thing about the Elgg file system is that it lets you keep the files under a directory structure. To further assist you and others in locating the file, Elgg lets you set attributes like titles and descriptions to the files and folders.

Find People

Connecting to other people is the whole purpose of social networking software. Elgg does its bit by providing you with a couple of ways to connect to other people and share resources. The foremost is the search box.

On Ubuntero, you'll find the search box on the top right-hand corner of the page. Enter a subject you are interested in, and Elgg will take care of the rest. By default, Elgg matches the search string with results from both the list of people and communities. But you can restrict Elgg to search either one of the two, by selecting them from the drop-down list.

If you don't have a particular search string in mind, or feel like wandering around, click on the **Browse** button. This will take you to the Elgg browser, which lists all users and communities registered with Ubuntero. Some statistics, like the numbers of blog posts and a brief description about the users and communities, are also displayed. Like with the search box, you can choose to display only users or communities.

Browser

Browse :: All | Users | Communities |

Filter : [   ] Filter >> |

Show icons	Name	Description	Connections	Posts	Type
	Ubuntero.org Admin		1276	6	person
	Ubuntu Brasil		38	2	community
	Ken Wilson	Ubuntero Developer	24	3	person
	Edwin Soto	Ubuntero Developer	23	3	person
	Andrew Conkling	Ubuntero Developer	23	0	person
	Game Development	A community about developing and bringing new games to ubuntu.	15	0	community
	Deanna	Ubuntu Supporter - aka Dark Wing Duck!	15	0	person
	Sipes	Male	competetive	Lover of all that is good	14	0	person
	Justin M. Wray	Security Evangelist. Linux Enthusiast	12	2	person
	Security Specialists	Information Security Specialists	11	2	community
	Oscar M. Cantu	Oscar. Programmer. Gamer. Dreamer.	10	3	person

Another option to look for topics is by using the **Tag Cloud** option. A Tag cloud is made up of the various popular keywords people are associating with their blog posts. The more popular tags are shown in a bigger font. Once you click on a tag, Elgg will guide you to a page that lists blog posts made in that category, people who have that category in their spaces, and so on. Elgg will also suggest other tags that it feels are similar to the tag you've selected.

Some Tags

The following is a selection of keywords used within this site. Click one to see related users, weblog posts or objects.

Manga, theology, rev. run, cooking, Germany, Rock climbing, Sleep, School, Languages, TV, Blogging, hacking, Italy, jme, Infodomestic Developer Connection Network, US, freeware, reading, ohio linuxfest, Colombia, ubuntu django python geek bioinformatics, JavaScript, mossad, boston, GNU/Linux, Indiana,

---

Yet another option to find people with similar interests is through your profile page. Remember I mentioned that Elgg turns your interests, likes and dislikes into links? You can click on one of these links to find people you share similar interests with, or like or dislike the same things as you!

Make Friends

Once you've found people or resources (like communities) through the search box or using your profile, the next step is to find out more about them. Click on a person's icon to find out details about them. You'll get information from their profile that they've made accessible to the public.

In addition to details on their profiles, you'll also be able to access to their blog, their files, and communities. Of course only those resources that they've cared to make public.

Once you've seen and read enough about a person, and they seem to be interesting enough to connect to, it's time to add them to your list of connections. Connecting to people and other users is the first step towards building your network.

Click here to add this user as a friend.Send Message

To add a user to your network, you get two options. You can either click on **Send Message** to send an email to the user, introducing yourself and sharing your willingness to join the user as a friend, or you can use the **Click here to add this user as a friend** link and Elgg will take care of the rest.

Your Community

Another way to talk about a topic that's dear to you is to form a community around it. Communities are formed around shared interests. For example, on Eduspaces.net, you'd have found communities that were virtual study groups. Research students formed communities to collaborate on their particular field of work. A community is a great way to bring together people and resources who share the same passion for a topic.

Once you've formed a community, you can then invite people to join in. It'll also show up in search results, which further helps you collate members. All members in a community can contribute. Each community is equipped with its own community blog, file repository, Wiki, syndication, and access privileges.

The **Communities** page on Elgg lists not only communities you've formed, but also communities you are a part of. From this page, you can also send an invitation to your friends to join the community and approve invitations to join other communities.

Your Messages

Elgg also has its own emailing software to enable communication between members. You can use the software to send messages to your friends on the network or even to communities.

Inbox			
Action: Select an action			
	Sent by	Subject	Date
1 ☐	Mayank Sharma	Test Message	07/05/2007, 20:39
2 ☐	?	New EduSpaces friend	07/05/2007, 20:39

We've already seen how you can find people that share the same interests or write about the topics that interest you. On the flip side, when someone comes across your profile, either by searching for topics or through the links on their profiles, they have the option to send messages to you. These messages show up in your inbox, along with the name of the person who has sent the message, the subject, and the date and time the message was sent.

Mayank Sharma :: Messages

View Messages | Compose | Sent Messages

New message

From:

Mayank Sharma

To:

Ubuntu India (Community)

Subject:

Test Message

Message:

Hi community. I am new to Elgg and Ubuntero.

Path:

Send

Like any other email service, Elgg also keeps track of messages you've sent to others using this facility. The system also gives you the ability to delete the messages or mark them as read or unread.

Your Resources

You can also easily keep track of resources that interest you on the network. Once you've found a resource, either through the search box or through your profile, you'd want to be connected to it to keep yourself updated.

Feeds | Publish to blog | View aggregator | Popular Feeds

Feeds are information streams from other sites. You will often see a link to an 'RSS' feed while browsing; enter the link address into the 'add feed' box at the bottom of the page to read that information from within your learning landscape.

Last updated	Resource name	
January 13 2008, 13:59	IT Manager's Journal :: Feature	View content	Unsubscribe
January 13 2008, 13:58	Linux.com :: Features	View content	Unsubscribe
January 13 2008, 13:58	OSNews	View content	Unsubscribe
	Update	Subscription list as OPML

To subscribe to a new feed, enter its address below:

| http:// | Subscribe |

Elgg helps you here by letting you subscribe to a resources' feed. This makes sure you're updated as soon as the resource itself is updated. A feed eradicates the need to manually look for the resource each and every time you're on the network.

Elgg also lets you subscribe to feeds of resources that are not on the network itself. For example, you can subscribe to Linux.com's article feed on Ubuntero.

Popular feeds

Feeds | Publish to blog | View aggregator | Popular Feeds

Feeds are information streams from other sites. You will often see a link to an 'RSS' feed while browsing; enter the link address into the 'add feed' box at the bottom of the page to read that information from within your learning landscape.

This is a list of the feeds with the most subscribers.

Last updated	Link to site	
January 13 2008, 08:17	Digg	View posts	Subscribe 6 Subscribers
January 13 2008, 10:07	Edwin Soto's Blog	View posts	Subscribe 3 Subscribers
January 13 2008, 04:11	Penguicon	View posts	Subscribe 3 Subscribers
January 11 2008, 23:47	Andrew's shared items in Google Reader	View posts	Subscribe 2 Subscribers
January 13 2008, 08:12	AppleGeeks	View posts	Subscribe 2 Subscribers

Elgg also keeps track of the most popular feeds off the network. The **Popular Feeds** link lists all the feeds with the most subscribers. It also keeps track of the date and time the feed was last updated, and the link to the site from where the feed originates. You also get the option to view the posts on the feed before subscribing to it.

Your Presentation

A presentation is a special type of content collation provided by Elgg. You can use a presentation to describe an individual or even a community. It's made up of several content sections. These content sections can contain either text, or content from a blog post, or even uploaded files from your repository.

Dave Tosh :: View Presentation

Plain View | Index

In the beginning - the first phase of Elgg 2004-2005

Contents

In the beginning

Elgg was started by Ben Werdmuller and I back in 2004 after writing a couple of draft papers looking at the integration of social technologies into ePortfolios, it has been quite a journey with some highs and many lows.

Here is part one; the early years 2004-2005.

0 Section Comments | Top

File: ePortfolios and weblogs: one vision for ePortfolio development

This was the first draft paper we wrote; it was well received and ended up being download 30,000 times.

We approached the department where I worked to see if there was any chance we could work on this and try to get it published in a journal (not in the form you see here, which is a draft) anyway, the answer was no. The funny thing is that had it been published instead of us releasing it via our blogs it would never have been read by so many people and subsequently Elgg might not have happened.

Title: ePortfolios and weblogs: one vision for ePortfolio development
Description: A draft paper discussing the possible benefits of weblog technology in e-portfolios.
Keywords: draft paper, eportfolios, weblogs
Size: 101548 bytes
Original filename: ePortfolio_Weblog.pdf

Imported at: 23/03/2007 13:34 GMT
The original file this was imported from is here.

Adding a section to a presentation isn't unlike writing a blog post. When writing static content, you need to divide it between a title and a body. When importing a blog post, or a file, you can add comments to describe the resource if you want.

Recent Activity

If you've been on vacation or busy with something that's kept you away from your Elgg network, you can quickly glance at what has transpired while you were away. The **Recent activity** link keeps track of all the action on your space within several time frames. There are links to break up activity between the last 24 hours, last 48 hours, the last week, and the last month.

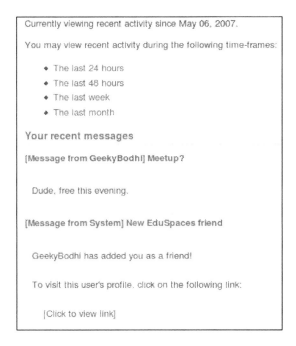

The page also lists recent messages that have landed in your inbox. Elgg can also keep track of activity on posts that you have marked as interesting. If someone has commented on the posts, you'll find the comment as soon as you return to your network.

Summary

In this chapter, we've looked at various aspects of an Elgg installation that we, as users, can influence and control. I've used publicly accessible Elgg-installations like the upcoming network of Ubuntu users, developers, and fans, Ubuntero.org, and the Elgg.org website itself, as examples to enable all of you to witness the screens and options first-hand. There's no dearth of Elgg installations available on the Internet, but because Elgg.org is run by the developers of Elgg, it's very close to a default Elgg installation that we'll deal with, later on in the book.

This chapter also serves as an extended and detailed feature-list of Elgg. After reading through the chapter, you should have a fairly good idea of what your very own Elgg-based social network should be capable of. To recap, you get a detailed profile builder, comprehensive friend management, file repository with directory structure, integrated blogging engine, email service, full fletched community management, and more, in one neat package.

3
Users, Profiles, and Connections

Ever been to a night club on a Monday morning? There's you, there are the chairs, and the potential to host a party on the weekend. If you've been through Appendix A, your Elgg installation looks pretty much like an empty night club. There are lots of buttons, lots of potential, but no member except you.

But unlike a night club, you don't have to wait for the weekend to host your friends on Elgg. Invite them as soon as you're done setting up the software.

Elgg is designed to make it easier for you to invite people. If you've ever setup a blog or rolled your own website, how long did it take before you could invite your friends over? You had to put up all sorts of content to indulge them, and also fiddle around decorating the portal so that it doesn't look dull.

That's where a social network is different from a regular website. The websites follow a two-way, one-to-many style of interaction, where the owner of the website, or blog, talks to all his visitors who respond with their comments, either on the website, or via e-mail.

On the other hand, social networking software follows a many-to-many style of interaction. Members interact with each other, and create their own content, which is then shared with all. This is then discussed and commented on by everyone.

The owner of the site is like the perfect host. They mingle, discuss with everyone, but don't stamp their authority, unless you're naughty. They're like every other member, except for the fact that they own the place. Sounds familiar?

So, you don't have to worry about content before inviting your friends. Your friends bring their own content. And thanks to Elgg's customization features, which I briefly touched upon in Chapter 2, members can customize their respective areas on the network as they please. Groovy!

Connecting to Friends and Users

I hope you're convinced how important friends are to a social network. Initially, you'll have to manually invite your friends over to join. I say initially, because membership on a social network is viral. Once your friends are registered members of your network, they can also bring in their own friends.

This means that soon your friends would have invited their own friends as well. Chances are that you might not know these friends of your friends. So, Elgg not only allows you to invite friends from outside, but also connect with users already on the network.

Let's understand these situations in real-life terms. You invite your friends over to a party with you at your new Star Trek theme club. That's what you'll do with Elgg, initially. So your friends like the place and next time around they bring in more friends from work. These friends of friends from work, talk about your place with their friends and so on, until you're hosting a bunch of people in the club that you haven't ever met in your life. You overhear some people discussing Geordi La Forge, your favorite character from the show. You invite them over for drinks. That's connecting with users already on the network.

So let's head on over to Elgg and invite some friends!

Inviting Friends to Join

There are two ways of inviting users to join your network. Either send them an email with a link to join the website, or let Elgg handle sending them emails.

If you send them emails, you can include a direct link to the registration page. This link is also on the front page of your network, which every visitor will see. It asks visitors to register an account if they like what's on the network. The procedure for registering using this mechanism has already been covered in Chapter 2.

Let Elgg Handle Registration

This is the most popular method of inviting users to join the network. It's accessible not only to you, but also to your friends once they've registered with the network. To allow Elgg to send emails on your behalf, you'll have to be logged into Elgg. This is covered as part of installation in Appendix A.

Once you login, click on the **Your Network** button on the top navigation bar. This will take you to a page, which links to tools that'll help you connect with others. The last link in this bar (**Invite a Friend**) does exactly what it says.

Invite a Friend

Communities | Owned Communities | Friends | Friend of | Friendship requests | FOAF | Access controls | Invite a friend

If you have a friend or colleague you would like to join the system, perhaps because you would like to share protected resources or reflections with them, you can enter their details below. They will then receive a special invitation email containing a code that allows them to create a new account; once they do so, a mutual friend connection will be created between their account and yours.

Their name

Docky Kolian

Their email address

honky.dory@myemail.net

An optional message

Hi Docky, I have just started this social network. Follow the link on this email and hop on!

Invite

When you click on this link, it'll explain to you some benefits of inviting friends over. The page has three fields:

- **Their name:** Enter the name of the friend you're sending the invitation to.
- **Their email address:** Very important. This is the address to where the invitation is sent.
- **An optional message:** Elgg sends an email composed using a template. If you want to add a personal message to Elgg's email, you can do so here.

In the email, which Elgg sends on behalf of the network's administrator, that means you, it displays the optional message (if you've sent one), along with a link to the registration page. The invitation is valid for seven days, after which the registration link in the email isn't valid.

When your friends click on the registration form, it asks them to enter their:

- **Name:** This is your friend's real name. When he arrives here by clicking the link in the email, this field already has the same name as the one in the email. Of course, your friend can choose to change it if he pleases.

- **Username:** The name your friend wants to use to log in to the network. Elgg automatically suggests one based on your friend's real name.

- **Password:** The last two fields ask your friend to enter (and then re-enter to confirm) a password. This is used along with the username to authenticate him on the system.

Once your friends enter all the details and click on join, Elgg creates an account for them, logs them in, and dispatches a message to them containing the log in details for reference.

Build a Profile

The first thing a new user has to do on the network is to create his profile. If you haven't yet built up a profile yourself, now is a good time.

Your profile has several purposes, which we've already covered in Chapter 2. To recap, your profile is your digital self. By filling in a form, Elgg helps you define yourself in terms that'll help other members find and connect to you.

This is again where socializing using Elgg outscores socializing in real life. You can find people with similar tastes, likes, and dislikes, as soon as you enter the network.

So let's steam ahead and create a digital you.

The Various Profile Options

Once you are logged into your Elgg network, select the **Your Profile** option from the top navigation-bar. In the page that opens, click the first link, **Edit this profile**.

This opens up a form, divided into five tabs—**Basic details, Location, Contact, Employment**, and **Education**. Each tab helps you fill in details regarding that particular area. You don't necessarily have to fill in each and every detail. And you definitely don't have to fill them all in one go.

Each tab has a **Save your profile** button at the end. When you press this button, Elgg updates your profile instantaneously. You can fill in as much detail as you want, and keep coming back to edit your profile and append new information.

This screen allows you to edit your profile. Blank fields will not show up on your profile screen in any view; you can change the access level for each piece of information in order to prevent it from falling into the wrong hands. For example, we strongly recommend you keep your address to yourself or a few trusted parties.

Basic details | Location | Contact | Employment | Education

Let's look at the various tabs:

- **Basic details**: Although filling information in any tab is optional, I'd advise you to fill in all details in this tab. This will make it easy, for you to find others, and for others to find you. The tab basically asks you to introduce yourself, list your interests, your likes, your dislikes, your goals in life, and your main skills.

- **Location**: This tab requests information that'll help members reach you physically. Fill in your street address, town, state, postal code, and country.

- **Contact**: Do you want members to contact you outside your Elgg network? This tab requests both physical as well as electronic means which members can use to get in touch with you. Physical details include your work, home, and mobile telephone number. Electronic details include your email address, your personal and official websites. Elgg can also list information to help users connect to you on instant messenger. It supports ICQ, MSN, AIM, Skype, and Jabber.

- **Employment**: List your occupation, the industry and company you work in, your job title and description. Elgg also lets you list your career goals and suggests you do so to "let colleagues and potential employers know what you'd like to get out of your career.".

- **Education**: Here you can specify your level of education, and which high school, university or college you attended, and the degree you hold.

As you can clearly see, Elgg's profiling options are very diverse and detailed. Rather than serve the sole purpose of describing you to the visitors, the profile also helps you find new friends as well, as we'll see later in this chapter.

What is FOAF?

While filling the profile, you must have noticed an **Upload a FOAF file** area down at the bottom of all tabs. FOAF or Friend of a Friend is a project (`http://www.foaf-project.org/`) to help create "machine-readable pages that describe people, the links between them and the things they create and do".

You can import some profile data by uploading a FOAF file here:

Upload a FOAF file:

| /home/bodhi/moi.xml | Browse... |

Upload

The FOAF file includes lots of details about you, and if you have already created a FOAF profile, Elgg can use that to pick out information describing you from in there. You can modify the information once it's imported into Elgg, if you feel the need to do so.

The FOAF-a-Matic tool (`http://www.ldodds.com/foaf/foaf-a-matic.en.html`) is a simple Web-based program you can use to create a FOAF profile.

A Face for Your Profile

Once you have created your digital self, why not give it a face as well. The default Elgg picture with a question mark doesn't look like you!

To upload your picture, head over to **Your Profile** and select the **Change site picture** link. From this page, click **Browse** to find and select the picture on your computer. Put in an optional description, and then choose to make it your default icon. When you click the **Upload new icon** button, Elgg will upload the picture.

Once the upload completes, Elgg will display the picture. Click the **Save** button to replace Elgg's default icon with this picture.

Mayank Sharma :: Manage user icons

Edit this profile | Change site picture

Site pictures

Site pictures are small pictures that act as a representative icon throughout the system.

Name: That's me!

Default: ⦿

Delete: ☐

Mayank Sharma

No default: ○

Save

Elgg will automatically resize your picture to fit into its small area. You should use a close-up of yourself, otherwise the picture will lose clarity when resizing. If you don't like the picture when it appears on the website, or you want to replace it with a new one, simply tick the **Delete** check-box associated with the picture you don't like. When you click **Save**, Elgg will revert to the default question-mark guy.

Access Control

You might be wondering what to do if you'd really like to share your physical address or home telephone number with each and every member on the network. Elgg has three pre-defined groups that help you share all information on the network, or keep them private.

The three groups are Private, Public, and Logged-in users. These can be associated with everything on the Elgg network, including profile items. By default, every profile item is visible only to users that are logged into the system. But it's very simple to change the access setting of a particular item.

Each and every profile item has a pull-down list with it. Use it to specify who gets to see a particular piece of information.

Access Restriction:
Public
Private
Public
Logged in users

You can also make some information, like your personal or company website, public, which means it's accessible by everyone, including non-registered members browsing the website. This is like pasting your website address on a window facing the street. Everyone can look at it.

For sure, you wouldn't want to do that with your mobile phone number. In fact, you might not want to share that with anyone on the network. Elgg helps you mark such information as private and keep them safe from everyone.

But what about information that you don't want anyone to see, except certain friends?

Define Your Own Control Lists

Elgg's default access controls are on the extreme sides. You can either share information with everyone on the network, or with no one.

To help create a middle ground, Elgg allows you to define your own access control groups. A custom access group is nothing but a list of your friends. So for example if you want to share your employment details with your colleagues from work, and not with your friends of friends you've just met, you can create a custom group called **colleagues** and only allow them to access your employment details.

For creating a custom group, head over to the **Your network** option. From here, click the **Access controls** button. On the page that opens, you'll be asked to enter the name of the group you want to create. Enter the name and click the **Create** button.

This will create the group and expand the page to list the groups you own. Under the name of the group, you'll notice two parallel columns. One lists all the friends you are connected with on the network, and the other lists friends in the group. To add your friends from work into the newly created **colleagues** group, simply select them from the friends list, by clicking on their name. To select multiple names, hold down the *Control* key (*Ctrl*), while selecting the names.

Once you are done selecting all the friends, click the **Add selected to group** button to add these friends to your custom group. If you, by mistake, added a friend that you don't want in this group, simply select him in the right-hand column, and click the **Remove selected from group** button.

```
Create a new group
Group name: [            ]   [ Create ]

Groups you own

[colleagues          ]   [ Save this group ]   [ Delete this group ]

Your friends:                Members of this group:
┌─────────────────┐          ┌─────────────────┐
│ Docky Malcoa    │          │ George Oswell   │
│ Karan Minhas    │          │ John Roberts    │
│ Karthik R.      │          │ Kerry Ryan      │
│                 │          │                 │
└─────────────────┘          └─────────────────┘
  [ Add selected to group ]    [ Remove selected from group ]
```

Once you've added all your friends from work to this group, click the **Save this group** button. Elgg will refresh the page and let you know that the group was updated. This means your custom group now lists all your friends from work.

After you've created the group, return to the profile page. Here you'll notice that the access restriction pull-down menu now lists your custom group as well. In case you are wondering, Elgg allows you to create as many groups as you like. You can customize the list of your friends in the group any time or even delete the group entirely.

```
Access Restriction:
[ Public              ▼]
  Private
  Public
  Logged in users
  Group: Close friends
  Group: colleagues
  Group: Just met
```

Making Friends with Internal Members

By now, you should have gotten a hang of navigating around in Elgg. You've populated your profile, and invited friends to join your network. As the word spreads about your network, members will start trickling in. Soon, you'll have a sizable number of people, all interested in the topic your network caters to.

It's not out of this world to imagine that you'll not know each and every one of them. Sure they are on your network, but the very nature of socializing on the Internet is to attract as many users as possible. Connections can happen, later.

So now that you have a dozen, or a hundred, or even a thousand members on your network, a majority of whom you don't know, how about making new friends?

Use Your Profile to Find Connections

When you log in, you are on the main welcome page. Here, you'll notice a link to view your profile. When you click on the link, you'll be taken to a page that lists all elements of your profile, along with the same two links to edit the profile, and change your site picture. Nothing fancy here, eh?

Wrong! Look closely.

You'll notice that some or all of your items listed under interests, likes, dislikes, goals, and skills have mysteriously turned blue. No, they aren't dead. They've transformed themselves into hyperlinks. This means these items are now clickable.

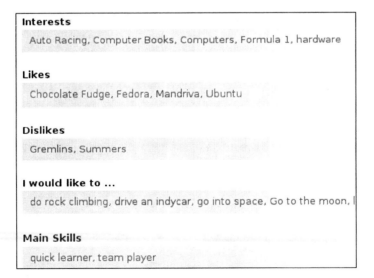

Interests

Auto Racing, Computer Books, Computers, Formula 1, hardware

Likes

Chocolate Fudge, Fedora, Mandriva, Ubuntu

Dislikes

Gremlins, Summers

I would like to ...

do rock climbing, drive an indycar, go into space, Go to the moon, l

Main Skills

quick learner, team player

Click on any one of them, and you are flown to a page that lists members who have the same entry in their profile.

For example, if you list 'chocolate fudge' as one of the things you like, it'll be converted into a hyperlink as soon as someone else lists it too. Now when you click on the link, you land up on a page that lists everyone who has listed 'chocolate fudge' in their respective 'likes' category in their profile.

Making Connections

Once Elgg finds other members who share the same tastes as you, it's very easy to find out more about them. Simply click on the person's icon or his name, and you'll be taken to his profile page. Here, you can browse items on his profile that he's made available for all logged in members to see.

Also, depending on what he's allowed you access to, you can, among other things, browse his blog, check out his friends, and his files.

After checking out the member, you can easily connect to him. In his right-side column, you'll notice a link that reads, **Click here to add this user as a friend**. When you do as it says, Elgg will confirm if you really want to add the user as a friend. Confirm your action, to list the user as your friend.

Once you're connected, the member will be listed under your friend's list.

By default, you'll still only share those details with this friend that all logged in users have access to. But if you want, you can choose to share some more information with the user, now that you are connected. The best way to do this is to create a custom group for new friends, where you share a little more information than is accessible to every logged in member.

Being connected also facilitates easier communication and sharing between the users as we'll see in later chapters, when we create specialized communities and share resources.

Friendship Moderation

This act of connecting to other users also raises an issue. Suppose a person on your network, comes across your profile, browses your blog, your profile, and decides to connect to you as a friend. Wouldn't you want to reserve the right to "approve" his friendship? He has had a chance to browse through your profile, and you should have the right to do that as well.

This is where Friendship moderation comes into play. We've gone over this option in Appendix A. The choice you made there, while setting up Elgg, were applicable to the entire system.

Let's suppose you left the default choice of "No moderation", to let anyone add anyone as their friend. You did that because most people would like that option. But you don't like the idea very much.

To change your friendship moderation setting, click on the **Account settings** option in the top navigation bar. From the page that opens, scroll down to the **Friendship moderation** option (third from the top). It has a pull-down menu that offers these three options:

- **No Moderation**: anyone can list you as a friend
- **Moderation**: friendships must be approved by you
- **Private**: nobody can list you as a friend

> Mayank Sharma has elected to moderate friendship requests. Your request has been added to their moderation queue.

The options are self-explanatory. Select the option that best suits you. If you decide to moderate your friend's requests, whenever a member tries to add you as a friend, Elgg will inform them that the user they're trying to connect with "**has elected to moderate friendship requests.**" Their requests will be added to your friendship moderation queue.

Managing Friendship Requests

Once you've decided to moderate your friendship requests, as soon as someone decides to add you as their friend, Elgg dispatches a message to you. To view these messages or friendship requests, head over to **Your Network**. Here, you'll notice the **Friendship requests** link.

This page houses all your friendship requests, along with these pieces of information:

- The user's picture
- The user's name
- Their brief description
- Link to their full profile
- Link to their blog

That's exactly what you wanted right? An equal opportunity to browse through your new friend's profile and blog. Once you've gone through these, it's time to make a decision. You can either accept the request to connect with the user, or decline to do so. Just click on the appropriate option.

The following users would like to add you as a friend. They need your approval to do this (to change this setting, visit the 'account settings' page).

Shashank Sharma   Approve | Decline

Shashank Sharma writes on open source development in India. He lives in New Delhi.

Profile | Blog

What's Friend Of?

You might have noticed the **Friend Of?** option listed under the **Your Network** section. Unlike the **Friends** option, which lists your friends on the network, the **Friend Of** option lists those members on whose "Friends" list you are on. Most of the time, both of these will list the same members. This is because there is no friendship moderation. All friend requests are instantaneously approved, and you also feature on your friends list.

The similarities end, when a user has friendship moderation turned on. In this case, when you accept a user's request to become your friend, he shows up only under your **Friend Of** option. On the contrary, for the user that sent you the request, you are only listed under **Friends**.

Other Account Settings

Apart from controlling friendship moderation, the account settings page also lets you make several changes to your accounts. You can:

- Change your full name
- Change your email address
- Change you password
- Make comments public: This controls who gets to comment on your resources. By default, it's restricted to logged in users only, but you can allow non-registered visitors to comment as well.
- Receive email notifications: Remember in Chapter 2, I briefly mentioned Elgg's email feature? You can choose to be alerted of any new messages in your Elgg email. If you do so, Elgg will send a small message to your regular email ID, mentioned above, saying that you have a new message on Elgg.
- Language selection: Choose from more than a dozen languages. The default is English.
- Visual text editing: Elgg has a built-in WYSIWYG (What You See Is What You Get) text editor that helps you compose your blog posts better. By default, it's turned on, but if you want, you can choose to turn it off.

Attracting Visitors

So far, we've only connected with friends who we invited ourselves or users that our friends invited. As your social network becomes popular, random visitors browsing the Internet might start showing up at our network's virtual doorstep.

Elgg has special mechanisms to entice visitors into registering. By giving visitors a sneak-peak of the content on the network, Elgg ensures that only interested people join. Previewing the content on the network also helps filter out people who might have come to the site expecting something else. This helps maintain the integrity of the network and ensure that the discussions are to the point.

Welcoming Guests

When visitors land up on your main page, they are greeted by Elgg's customized welcome message. It describes the network as per the settings covered in Appendix A. In addition to describing the network, Elgg also lists three links to help visitors make a decision regarding registration.

Please remember, Elgg only shares that information that is made accessible to the public. Private posts, posts made accessible to logged in members, or to custom groups, will not be listed on this page.

These details are on the page:

> ## Welcome Guest
>
> This is My Elgg site, a learning landscape. Why not check out what people are saying right now?
>
> Find others with similar interests and goals.
>
> Here are some example users: Shashank Sharma
>
> If you like what you see, why not register for an account?

- **What people are saying**: This is the first link and gives visitors a sneak peak on the blog posts made by registered users. Visitors get an idea of what the members like to discuss, and what are they passionate about.

- **Find others with similar interests and goals**: This link takes visitors to a page where all keywords that describe interests, likes, dislikes, and so on, marked by more than one member are listed. This helps visitors get an idea of the categories of topics discussed in the network.

- **Example users**: There's no better way to find out about the network, than to view profiles of its members. Elgg lists several members here that have some items on their profile that members of the public can access. By clicking on the sample user's name, the visitor can, not only access their profile, but also their blog, and posts. Of course, only those items that are publicly accessible.

> ## Some Tags
>
> The following is a selection of keywords used within this site. Click one to see related users, weblog posts or objects.
>
> Ubuntu, do rock climbing, Auto Racing, Computers, Summers, Fedora, Chocolate Fudge, hardware, team player, go into space

Administration Options

So far all the options we've covered are also accessible to other members on the site. But you are the owner, the gracious host, the head honcho. You have special powers and it's time to look at some of them now.

Administration

Main | Add users | Manage users | Manage flagged content | Spam control

Site statistics

Weblog statistics	**All-time:** 1 weblog posts, 0 comments
	Last 7 days: 0 weblog posts, 0 comments
File statistics	**All-time:** 0 files (bytes)
	Last 7 days: 0 files (bytes)
Database statistics	**Total database size:** 102970 bytes

While all accounts on an Elgg network look the same, you'll notice the **Administration** link at the top navigation bar. Only you have this link, which allows you to control various aspects of the site. Let's look at some of these aspects that involve users.

Add Users in Bulk

Earlier in the chapter, we've looked at how you can invite your friends to join the network. But there's an easier, administrative way of inviting friends.

Add multiple users

Main | Add users | Manage users | Manage flagged content | Spam control

You can create up to 12 users below; passwords will be autogenerated and emailed to the account owners. You must include all fields, but you may leave rows blank.

Username	Full name	Email address
koko	Kapital Jr.	kokokap@myemail.net
luther	Joe Random	jorra@yousaid.org
chico	George Oswell	who.me@ond.com
red	Karan Minhas	who.me4@ond.com
clay	Karthik R.	who.me5@ond.com

Add users

From the administration screen, select the **Add users** option. This opens a page which allows you to register up to 12 users in one go. Acting on behalf of the users, enter these details:

- Username
- Full name
- Email address

Once you're done filling up these details, click on the **Add users** button. Elgg will automatically generate a password for these users, and dispatch an email to them with the details. The email, sent on your behalf, informs the user that they've been added to your Elgg network. It also lists the username (which you specified) and the password (which Elgg auto generated).

The user can then follow the link in the email to log in to the network. Once inside, a user can change his settings, including username and password, as mentioned in the account settings section above.

Change User Settings

As the administrator of the Elgg network, you can view all members connected to the site. On top of that, you can change several settings of any user.

To do so, from the administration panel, head over to the **Manage users** link. This page lists all users on the network, 50 per page. To change settings of a particular user, you can either look for him in the list or simply enter his username, if you are aware of it.

Manage users

Main | Add users | Manage users | Manage flagged content | Spam control

The following is a list of all the users in the system, 50 users at a time. You can click each one to edit their user details as if you were logged in as them, as well as set user flags (including 'ban user' and 'set user as administrator').

If you know the username of the user you would like to edit, you can also enter it below.

Enter username		Edit user
Username	**Full name**	**Email address**
chico	George Oswell [Profile]	who.me@ond.com
clay	Karthik R. [Profile]	who.me5@ond.com
docko	Docky Malcoa [Profile]	geeky_bodhi@yahoo.co.in
geekybodhi	Mayank Sharma [Profile]	geekybodhi@gmail.com
news	News [Profile]	geekybodhi@gmail.com
orion	John Roberts [Profile]	who.me2@ond.com
red	Karan Minhas [Profile]	who.me4@ond.com
shashanks	Shashank Sharma [Profile]	linuxlala@gmail.com
tauras	Kerry Ryan [Profile]	who.me3@ond.com
testuser	Test User [Profile]	geekybodhi@gmail.com

Once you do so, you are taken to that particular user's account settings page. But this one's a little different. Apart from their account settings, you can modify these settings:

- **Change file quota**: This field lets you specify, in bytes, the total size of files a user can upload onto the network.
- **Change icon quota**: This is the size of the icons the user can upload on to the network.
- **User flags**: Using this option, you can share your site administrator privileges with another user.
- **Banned**: Finally, if you think the user is contaminating the discussions on the network, or acting naughty, you can ban him from logging into the network.

Change file quota (in bytes):

New file quota:

1000000000

Change icon quota:

New icon quota:

10

User flags:

Site administrator:

◯ Yes ⦿ No

Banned:

◯ Yes ⦿ No

Once you've made all the choices, click on save to update the user's settings.

Playing Boss

Till now, we've toured and implemented some of the Elgg settings related to users, profiles, and connections. They all look good in theory, especially when our network is small. But when you are managing an Elgg network with dozens of users, you'll have to think out of the box. Understanding how to use an option is only part of the solution. To harness its power, you have to know what an option is capable of.

The settings below might sound pervasive to some users. Some will also be flabbergasted because we discuss restricting users on our social network. It's important to understand that while creating content is the primary objective of a social network, we wouldn't want users to contaminate our system with off-topic or illegal discussions.

Blocking Users

As you are running a social network, there will be a lot of people who'll misuse the moderation-free environment to abuse the system. If while installing, you had set up Elgg to allow anyone to register, there will be people who'll register with the sole purpose of distracting others.

In the chapter on content creation, we'll see how Elgg can help you keep the discussions on topic. Once you've spotted a user with a history of interfering in discussions and taking them off-topic or uploading blog posts and files that violate your policy, it's time to kick the miscreant from the network.

1. Log in to your Elgg account and click the **Administration** link.
2. From the administration panel, click the **Manage Users** link. This will bring up a list of users on the system.
3. Select the user who's abusing the system or enter his username in the space provided, and click on **Edit user** button. This will take you to a page from where you can edit that user's details.
4. Scroll down to the **User flags:** section. Under the **Banned:** option, toggle the **Yes** radio button to ban the user.
5. Click the **Save** button to save these settings.

Once a user is banned, he'll not be able to log in to the network. When the banned user returns to the network and tries to log in, he'll receive the **You have been banned from the system!** message.

Can I Formally Warn Users?

Sometimes, it's not necessary that a user takes the discussion off-topic on purpose. Maybe he isn't really aware of the network's policy. As an admin, you should have the power to warn the user that he's taking the discussion off-topic, and he should mend his ways. Else, you'll have no option but to ban him.

Currently, Elgg lacks such a warning system. But you can still manually warn the user. Because as an admin, you have the user's email address, you can email him with links to the content that you have found to be inappropriate.

Removing the Ban

If a user promises to mend his ways and stick to the network's guidelines, you can restore his account. When you ban a user, Elgg doesn't remove the user from the system. Neither is any of his content automatically deleted.

To enable a banned account:

1. Log into your Elgg account and click the **Administration** link.
2. From the administration panel, click the **Manage Users** link. This will bring up a list of users on the system.
3. Select the user whose account you want to re-instate or enter his username in the space provided, and click on **Edit user** button. This will take you to a page from where you can edit that user's details.
4. Scroll down to the **User flags:** section. Under the **Banned:** option, toggle the **No** radio button to ban the user.
5. Click the **Save** button to save these settings.

This should re-instate the user's status on the system, and they'll be able to log in with their original username and password.

Limiting Users on the Site

As Elgg helps you create small specialized networks, unlike the bigger more generalized ones like MySpace, it makes sense to restrict the amount of resources a member can use. Because resources on a server are expensive, you wouldn't want members to upload all their music collection or tons of pictures.

Changing Space Quota

Elgg lets you vary the space allotted to each member. The best policy would be to keep it to an absolute minimum and let members request from you additional space if they want to upload something that's very useful and relevant to all members.

There isn't any built-in mechanism in Elgg to let members request you to increase their space. They'll have to rely on email to inform you.

The way this works is pretty simple:

1. Log into your Elgg account and click the **Administration** link.
2. From the administration panel, click the **Manage Users** link. This will bring up a list of users on the system.

3. Select the user whose resource you want to limit or enter his username in the space provided and click on the **Edit user** button. This will take you to a page from where you can edit that user's details.

4. Scroll down to the **Change file quota** section. Enter the new file quota in the space provided, replacing the number in the box.

5. Click the **Save** button, to save these settings.

Note that the space is mentioned in bytes. The default figure of 1000000000 bytes is almost 954 MB! Use Google's search bar to convert a figure in MB or KB into bytes. 5 MB is 5242880 bytes.

Sharing Admin Rights

As your Elgg network grows, it might not be feasible for you to manage it all by yourself. In any case, even if a network has only a few users, sharing administration privileges with a trusted user would make your task a little easier. Carefully choose the member you wish to share the administration duties with:

1. Log into your Elgg account and click the **Administration** link.

2. From the administration panel, click the **Manage Users** link. This will bring up a list of users on the system.

3. Select the user with whom you wish to share administrative powers or enter his username in the space provided and click on **Edit user** button. This will take you to a page from where you can edit that user's details.

4. Scroll down to the **User flags:** section. Under the **Site administrator**: option, toggle the **Yes** radio button to escalate the user's power to that of a Elgg administrator.

5. Click the **Save** button to save these settings.

The Scope of an Elgg Administrator

An Elgg administrator has full control of the network. He shares the same privileges as the person who has set up the network.

While this is a good option in certain situations, it's overkill in others. For example, let's consider you are running Elgg to connect students in your school. You will have no issues sharing the administration duties with a colleague.

But it's possible every class or subject has a forum of their own, or maybe run a multi-member blog. Since managing these dozens of forums and blogs would be difficult for you, it's only natural for you to appoint the class monitor to look over the respective blog or forum. But would you really want to share the full administrative powers with this student?

Unfortunately, Elgg currently doesn't let the main administrator define the scope of the administrative powers for another user. There are only two types of users: normal users with no control over the Elgg network, or site administrators with complete control of the network.

But Elgg is still evolving. It's under heavy development and some of the features that it's not capable of currently, will probably be introduced in future versions of Elgg.

Some of the settings we've covered in this chapter are very powerful, and an improper setting can prevent users from entering the network. Please exercise caution while playing around with these settings, and if possible, first try them out on a test user.

Summary

In this chapter, we've covered the most important aspect of a social network—the users. We've discussed several ways of inviting users to join the network. Some are more direct methods, which can be replicated by other users as well, while others can only be used by us, the administrators.

Getting the user to the site is only one aspect of socializing. The other important aspect is creating his online portfolio or profile. The profile quantifies the user in certain pre-determined criteria. In addition to describing him, we've seen how the profile also helps the user find people with similar tastes.

As the profile lists several vital and sensitive pieces of information, privacy concerns have been addressed in this chapter. We've seen the various built-in options that Elgg provides, as well as the mechanism to create our own custom groups.

Then, we've covered how one can connect with other users on the network. Again, privacy concerns have been addressed, followed by a discussion about moderating friendship requests. We also ran through Elgg's built-in mechanisms for attracting visitors to join the network, and various account settings that a user can alter.

After reading this chapter, you should have no trouble adding, managing or connecting to members in your Elgg network.

4
Blogging and Resources

Riddle me this: In a social network, what's as important as making friends? Yes, you got it—creating content!

I hope I don't have to rely on the old bookish saying that in the information age content is king. If you use the Internet to look up information about your washing machine, read an online manual, and when all else fails, send an email to the service department, you know the importance of content.

You can have the entire population of the world on your social network, but if they don't generate content, they aren't helping the cause. Interaction is an important aspect of a social network. When you sign up for public speaking, you don't go up on stage, shake hands, and just make friends.

As an administrator, it's your responsibility to encourage members to contribute. Elgg makes your task easier by providing several tools for generating and sharing content. Furthermore, it also offers tools to help you manage the content and keep it within the scope of the network.

Handling Files

Files play an important part of our Elgg social network. As we've seen in previous sections and chapters, we can embed files in blog posts or share them with other members. Of course, we can also control the amount of space allotted to individual users and communities for uploading files.

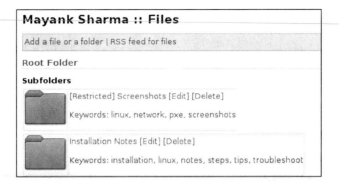

Elgg has special mechanisms for dealing with different formats of files. It also has a very friendly method for organizing stored files in folders. Elgg stores data hierarchically in folders. Starting with the Root folder, a folder can have several files or several folders, which can again have files or more folders and so on. Think of this arrangement as an inverted tree, with the roots at the top and the branches, representing files and folders, below.

Creating Folders

Files are managed through the **Your Files** section of Elgg. When you first enter that section, Elgg will inform you that the Root folder is empty. It also presents you with a form to upload files or create new folders.

The folder creation form has four fields:

- **Name**: The name of the folder.
- **Folder Type**: Elgg has two types of folders, one for storing images (**Photo Gallery**) and the other for storing all other types of files (**Default File Folder**). We'll discuss them in detail as we upload files in them.
- **Access Restriction**: By now, you should be absolutely clear about what this is. You can restrict access to the file, to Elgg's pre-defined groups, your custom groups of friends or even communities.
- **Keywords**: Just like in blogs, keywords make your files more searchable if that's what you want. If these folders are to hold private files, you can avoid listing keywords.

To create a folder, enter the name and keywords that describe the type of content inside the folder. You also have to choose the type of folder. By default, Elgg creates folders to hold documents. While you can store images in these folders as well, it's better to use the **Photo gallery** option when creating folders that'll hold images. Finally, specify who you want to share this folder with by selecting the appropriate user group from the pull-down menu.

Create a new folder

To create a new folder, enter its name:

Screenshots

Folder type:

Photo gallery ▾

Access restrictions:

Community: Linux "Network" Admins ▾

Keywords (comma separated):

linux, network, screenshots, pxe

Create

Uploading Files

The procedure for uploading files is the same, regardless of the types of folder you're uploading to. Before you can upload files, make sure you are inside the correct folder. By default, you are at the Root folder. To move into one of the folders we've created, simply click on the name of the folder, which is actually a hyperlink.

All the files you upload here will be uploaded into the current folder.

The file upload form has five fields:

- **File to upload**: The path to the file you want to upload.
- **File title**: Title of the file to help users identify it.
- **File description**: A description of the contents of the file.
- **Access restriction**: Controls the group of people who can view the file.
- **Keywords**: To make your file more searchable and show up in the tag cloud.

To upload a file, move into the folder that you want to keep the file under. Then, click on the **Browse** button to locate the file on your computer. Add a title and description to it. Choose the group that can access the file and add relevant keywords.

Upload a file

You have used 0 Mb of a total 10 Mb.

File to upload:	/home/bodhi/book.pdf Browse...
File title:	Installation Handbook
File Description:	This is a small (free) ebook that covers Linux installation.
Access restrictions:	Community: Linux "Network" Admins ▾
Keywords (comma separated):	linux, installation, ebook, book, newbie, install

☑ By checking this box, you are asserting that you have the legal right to share this file, and that you understand you are sharing it with other users of the system.

Upload

Right to Share

One thing you'd have noticed while uploading files is a checkbox at the bottom. The checkbox reads: **By checking this box, you are asserting that you have the legal right to share this file, and that you understand you are sharing it with other users of the system.**

This is quite self explanatory. As an administrator, you wouldn't want people to misuse the ability to upload files by sharing copyrighted files.

Viewing Files

Visitors to your profile have several ways of reaching your file repository. They can either get to them through your profile, or by finding them using the search box or tag cloud.

```
Folders owned by 'Mayank Sharma' in category 'linux'

    📁    Installation Notes


    📁    Screenshots


Files owned by Mayank Sharma in category 'linux'

         Customizing the network
         [In folder 'Installation Notes']

         Detailed instructions on customizing the network.

         IAS1741083.pdf

         Install instructions
         [In folder 'Installation Notes']

         Detailed step-by-step installation instructions.

         16315131.pdf

         Network Configuration Options
         [In folder 'Screenshots']

         Fedora's network configuration options.

         network_config.png

[ RSS feed for files owned by Mayank Sharma in category 'linux' ]
```

To view the files, visitors can click on the files and view them from the same page. But if the file they want to view is an image file in a folder of type **Photo gallery**, then the best way to view the file is to change into the parent folder.

As I mentioned earlier, a **Photo gallery** folder is a special type of folder for storing and displaying image files. When inside the folder, visitors get thumbnail previews of the images. On clicking, the images are displayed in a special JavaScript gallery. The background fades in to reveal the image in the foreground.

Moving and Deleting Files/Folders

You can easily move files from one folder to another or delete them altogether. If you are the owner of the files or folder, you'll notice two links next to them—**[Edit]** and **[Delete]**.

If you click the **Edit** link of a file, you'll be able to modify any of its five parameters — title, description, access restriction, keywords, and the folder they reside in. If you want to move the file to another folder, simply select the appropriate folder from the pull-down list. Or if you want to modify its description, type in a new one in the space provided. Once you are done making the changes, click on the **Save** button and Elgg will apply the changes.

Edit Network Configuration Options

File title:

Network Configuration Options

File description:

Fedora's network configuration options.

Access restrictions:

Public

File folder:

> Screenshots

Root
> Screenshots   linux, network
> Installation Notes

Keywords (comma separated):

Save

Similarly, if you click the edit link of a folder, you can change any of its five parameters as well — folder name, access restriction, keywords, type of folder, and parent folder. Once you have made the changes, click the **Save** button to apply them.

Deleting files or folders is pretty simple and straightforward. Just hit the delete button next to the file or the folder you want to remove.

Remember that when you delete a folder, Elgg only removes the folder and moves the files or folders under it to the parent folder of the folder being deleted. For example, suppose you have a folder called Podcasts under the Root folder. The Podcast folder holds several .OGG music files. Now, if you remove the Podcast folder, it will be deleted, but Elgg will move all the .OGG files to the Root folder.

Commenting on Files

If you have files that are accessible to others, either to the public or to restricted groups and communities, Elgg lets other users comment on them as well. Attaching comments to files is pretty useful. It allows users give their feedback on the shared file, which in turn helps other users decide whether they should download the file or not.

But that's just one aspect. If you are running a network for budding photographers, who share photographs, the ability to comment on files is a must-have feature.

Commenting on files isn't very difficult. Once users have located a file, on the bottom, Elgg displays a line that shows the number of comments on that particular file. It also invites users to click on this line to view the existing comments or add their own.

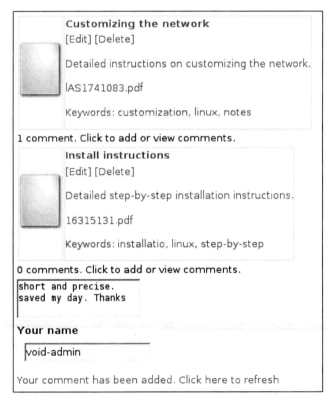

Start Blogging

There's no better way of generating content than with blogs. With Elgg, each member can have their own blog. Elgg's blogging software is feature rich. Not only does it support many features of standard blogging software, it makes it easier to find an audience and make friends.

You can control your blog, add posts, view archive and your friend's blog, and so on from the **Your Blog** section.

Posting a New Entry

You must be logged into your Elgg account to post a new entry. Head over to the **Your blog** section and click the **Post a new entry** link.

The page that opens has several fields. Let's look at them in detail:

- **Post Title**: This is the title of your blog post.
- **Add External Video**: You can easily import videos from popular websites like YouTube into your blog posts using this button.
- **Add File**: This is used to embed files we've stored on our personal space on the Elgg network.
- **Post body**: This is where you enter the main text of your post. This section also has some controls for controlling the formatting of the post.
- **Keywords**: Keywords are an important part of the post. Keywords are single words that define the content of post. Keywords appear on the tag cloud and are used to lure visitors to the post. They are also searchable.
- **Access Restrictions**: You're all familiar with the function of this drop down box. Using this box, you can control access to the blog post.

Add a new post

Post title:

Time to switch on SELinux?

Add External video | Add File

Post body:

B *I* <u>U</u> | ABC ≣ ≣ ≣ ≣ ≔ ⊞ ⊠ ↻ ⊂ ⊃ ⊗ HTML ◈ ▾ ☺

🔍 🔍 ↔

Between the two years, and 4 Fedora releases, a lot had changed. From a little-tested policy that worked best in a controlled, restricted environment but not at all well on a regular desktop, SELinux policies have evolved. And how! SELinux under FC6 has a new <u>Multi-Category Security policy</u>, there are <u>several graphical and command-line tools for analyzing policy and AVC audit messages</u>, and the <u>SELinux Troubleshooter</u> that detects denials and suggests fixes.

Now it looks like companies are starting to notice and helping users utilize the full potential of SELinux. <u>Hannes Kuehnemund from SAP recently wrote on his blog</u> that several SAP

Path:
p

Keywords (Separated by commas):
Keywords commonly referred to as 'Tags' are words that represent the weblog post you have just made. This will make it easier for others to search and find your posting.

fedora, linux, SAP, security, selinux

Access restrictions:

Logged in users ▾

Post

To make a blog post entry, just fill in the fields and click on the **Post** button. Elgg informs you that the post has been added to your weblog and returns you to the main **Your Blog** page. You can see your latest entry here.

Presto! You're a blogger!

Adding External Videos

With the proliferation of video sharing websites like YouTube, many people have started sharing video files in their blogs. Most people simply share the URL to the video. But with Elgg's blogging engine, you can embed the video in your blog post itself. Readers will be able to watch the video and control it (play/pause) without leaving your network. Cool, eh?

To embed a video, you'll need to do a little digging. You can't simply copy-paste the URL from the web browser's address bar. You'll have to hunt for the video's embed HTML code block. For example, a YouTube video's URL looks like `http://youtube.com/watch?v=EgrfmSm0NWs`, while the embed HTML block spans multiple lines and reads something like:

```
<object width="425" height="350"><param name="movie" value="http://
www.youtube.com/v/EgrfmSm0NWs"></param><param name="wmode"
value="transparent"></param><embed src="http://www.youtube.com/v/
EgrfmSm0NWs" type="application/x-shockwave-flash" wmode="transparent"
width="425" height="350"></embed></object>
```

Once you have the video's embed HTML code block, click on the **Add External Video** button from the **Add a new post** page. This will pop-up a small window with a form and two fields. Enter the embed HTML code in the field marked for **Video URL**. Elgg also lets you control the dimensions of the frame inside which the video will be played. By default, the size is 240x200 pixels but you can increase or decrease it as you please.

After entering the video details, click the **Insert video** button to embed the video in your post. Depending on your cursor's position inside the **Post body** text box, instead of the video, Elgg will append something that reads like `{{video:http://www.youtube.com/v/EgrfmSm0NWs@@240x200}}`. This is Elgg's way of letting the blogging engine know that it has to grab a video from YouTube and display within 240x200 pixels.

Embedding Files in Blogs

If you recall, while we were discussing how to post a new blog entry, I mentioned that you could embed files from your file repository in your posts as well. Now that we have a file repository, let's go back to our blog and use one of the files in our post.

When you head over to the blogging section to post a new entry, scroll to the **Add file** button. Clicking it will bring up a pop-up window that'll help you select a file to embed in your post. The window is divided into two panes. The left pane lists all the folders and sub-folders you have in your repository. When you click on a folder in the left pane, all files under it are listed in the right pane. To embed a file, simply click on the name of the file. Keep doing this until you've embedded all the files that you want to.

The pop-up isn't only useful for embedding files. You can also change folders and embed files of all types from your repository without leaving the pop-up. The pop-up window further assists by allowing you to upload a file into your repository and then embedding it into the post. The procedure for uploading a file is the same as we've already covered above.

Once you're done embedding files, close the pop-up window and return to the post. As with video files, instead of the file, you'll notice a simple piece of code inserted into your blog post's body. The code is actually a number enclosed in curly braces: {{file:5}}.

What Does the Number Mean?

Elgg assigns a unique number to each file and folder. You can view the number by hovering over a file in the **Your Files** section. The number will appear in the status bar of the browser.

So for example if you see something like **http://localhost/elgg/news/files/6/5/ lAS1741083.pdf**, this means the file **lAS1741083.pdf** is available from the user whose username is **news**. The file has the number 5 and is inside a folder with the number 6.

Saving Drafts

Sometimes, you wouldn't want to publish your blog post immediately. Like good coffee, some blog posts take time to brew. Actually, blog posts have nothing to do with coffee, but you get the idea, right? Maybe you want to spell check the post again in the morning. Maybe you want to add some external media file, which isn't available yet. For some reason, you just aren't in a mood to hit the post button just yet. What do you do?

Elgg offers you two options. One option requires a plug-in while the other can be used out of the box. Both options have their benefits. Let's take a closer look.

Mark Posts as Private

The quickest way to keep a work-in-progress to yourself, is to mark it as a private post. To do this, just post as you normally would, and when you are done for the time being, creating your master piece blog post, select the **Private** option from the pull-down **Access restrictions** menu.

Now your post is on the Elgg system but no one can see it and of course, it doesn't show up on the RSS feed either. But when you log into your blogging section, you'll see that post marked as **Private** post.

When you are in a mood to make some changes to the post, find it on the system, and click on the **Edit** link to edit the post just as you would any normal post. And just like before, when you're done making the updates, save the post as private post. Keep doing this until you think the world is ready for your blog post.

When you're ready to let loose the blog post, edit it like you've been doing all the while. But just before hitting the **Post** button, choose to make the post public. Or you can choose any other custom access restriction group you've created. The point is, when you want to publish a **draft** post, choose one of the access restriction lists that has more people on the list than just you.

So, Why Use a Plug-in?

This method of saving draft posts as private, seems quite useful. Why would anyone want to install and use a plug-in for something that can be done without one? It's because the method we've just discussed has some disadvantages.

The disadvantage of using the private method of saving drafts is that when you finally make your draft public, it appears beneath public posts that you've made after first saving the draft as private. For example, let's suppose you make a post titled Post #1 and save it as private. This is your draft. Now, you create another post titled Post #2 and release it into the wild. Now, you head back over to your first draft post, saved as private, make some changes, and now post it as public. In your blog and on the RSS feed, this post will appear in its original position, beneath the second post.

So, draft posts that make the transition from private to public, appear in the same order and place in the blog, in which they were made. There's a high probability that your readers might miss it. The other disadvantage is of course keeping track of private drafts. You have to manually search for posts marked as private throughout your blog to look for draft posts. Both these disadvantages turn ugly in a blog with a reasonable number of posts, like 20 or more. Scrolling through multiple pages of posts, the chances of you ever returning to draft posts are reduced considerably.

The Draft Post Plug-in

So you see, the first draft as private posts method is far from an optimal solution. The draft post plug-in not only provides the same convenience as the previous method, but removes its disadvantages.

With the draft post plug-in, whenever you head over to your blog to create a new post, it reminds you that you have posts marked as drafts and prints their titles. Secondly, when you get around to publishing draft posts, the plug-in identifies them as new posts to the blogging engine. This results in these posts being shown on the top of your blog and RSS feed.

To use the draft post plug-in, just download it (`http://www.elgg.org/mod/plugins/plugin.php?id=34`) and extract it's content under Elgg's `mod/` directory. That's it. When you now head over to your blog, while creating a new post, you'll notice a new addition to the **Access restriction** pull-down list called **Draft Post**. Just make sure you use this option, while saving drafts. Posts saved as drafts using this plug-in are marked as **Restricted**.

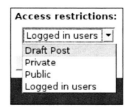

From this point, whenever you create a new post, a system message at the top of the screen will remind you of the draft posts. Publishing a draft post for public consumption is the same as with the previous technique. Just select a wider access restriction group.

Editing/Deleting Posts

Once a post is published, it's not cast in iron. In case you want to modify it, you can easily edit it to add/remove text or tags.

To edit an entry, log in and head over to the **Your Blog** section. Click on the **View blog** link and find the post you want to edit. At the bottom of the post, you'll notice a bunch of links. The links accompany the name of the user who has made the blog post. Next to this are links to **Edit** or **Delete** the post. Click on the appropriate link to either make changes to the post or remove it completely.

Posted by Mayank Sharma | Edit | Delete | 3 comment(s)

What Are Your Friends Blogging About?

Since you have friends on the network, shouldn't you get easier access to their blogs? You should and you do.

From the **Your Blog** section, you can see blog posts made by your friends — just click on the **Friends' blogs** link. The page lists posts made by your friends in descending chronological order, with the most recent post at the top.

Keeping Track of Posts and Discussions

So you're browsing through the network looking for posts or people interested in discussing technology. You head over to the search box, type in technology and see that there's a user who has a weblog post with the technology keyword.

You click on the link and Elgg prints out all the posts the user has under the technology category. Reading through one of the posts you realize that the post is interesting enough to keep track of. Especially, since the discussion in the comments section is pretty interesting and useful.

Elgg can not only help you track and locate posts that catch your fancy, but also help you stay informed of developments. To let it do so, open the post in question, scroll down to the bottom of the page. After all the comments you'll come to the **Keep track of this post** section. The section has a button to mark the post as interesting.

When you click on the **Mark interesting** button, the post will be added to your **interesting** list. The post will now be easily accessible from under the **Interesting posts** link.

Keep track of this post
Click the 'Mark interesting' button to monitor new comments on your 'recent activity' page.

Mark interesting

You can also keep track of the discussions on the post, from the **Recent Activity** section. Click on the **View your activity** link in the right-hand column. On the main page that tracks your recent activity, you'll notice a section that records **Activity on weblog posts you have marked as interesting**. It will, for example, list all the comments that have been added to the **interesting** posts since you've marked them.

Activity on weblog posts you have marked as interesting

ritmi commented on weblog post 'Interpreting a software license' in Shashank Sharma:

I wholeheartedly agree. I am really puzzled at how some developers in the kernel development team came to their conclusions. As if they hadn't read the license at all. That it so very sad and their style of discussion is kinda demagogically. Why? Don't get it.

Read more

Handling Improper Content

The biggest issue with decentralizing content creation is the odd-rogue member taking advantage of the moderation-free environment to inject impolite content. Freedom on big networks like Wikipedia, the free encyclopedia, is also constantly being abused. But like the software that powers Wikipedia, Elgg too has some mechanisms for dealing with content contamination.

The best way to avoid improper content from creeping into your network, is to moderate each and every blog post. But that's against the spirit of a social network and also impractical on a network with multiple contributors. The next best thing is to rely on users to report improper content.

Elgg allows members to flag objectionable content. As the administrator, you can review the content, warn the user to remove the content, or ban him from the network.

Flagging Improper Posts

Suppose someone stumbles upon a blog post that abuses your policy and has inappropriate content, they can mark the post as obscene. This is similar to marking the post as interesting, but the effect is opposite.

Marking a post is often referred to as flagging it. The first section of the blog post page, is the **Flag content** section. There, you'll notice the **Flag** button, which when clicked will notify you, the administrator.

Flag content

To mark this content as obscene or inappropriate, click the 'Flag' button and an administrator will view it in due course.

Flag

Elgg currently doesn't distinguish between normal and flagged posts. Ideally, it should warn other readers trying to read the post by displaying a notice that some users have found the post inappropriate and the administrators' action is awaited.

Managing Flagged Content

Once a post has been marked as flagged, it needs to be acted upon by the administrator, that means, you. Don your administrator cap and head over to admin section by clicking the **Administration** link on the top panel.

On the administration panel, click the **Manage flagged content** link. This displays a list of pages that some users have found objectionable. Additionally, the number of complaints that have been registered against the content is also displayed.

Now you have two options—to delete the content or to dismiss the complaints.

	Page URL	Number of objections
☐	/elgg/shashanks/weblog/3.html	2
	Remove flag(s)	

To delete the content, click on the link to the page. This takes you to the post. Since you are logged in as administrator, you have the power to edit the post or delete it. Select the appropriate action from below the post by clicking on either the **Edit** button or the **Delete** button.

In case you find nothing wrong in the flagged post, or the author has modified it, or it has been deleted, you can dismiss the complaint. From the **Content flags** section, click the checkbox next to the post that you want to dismiss and click the **Remove flag(s)** button. You can dismiss multiple complaints by clicking their respective checkboxes before hitting the **Remove flag(s)** button.

Filtering Blog Posts

We've already seen how you can keep track of blog posts made by your friends. Elgg also makes it easier to mark and watch over certain posts that you think are interesting. Furthermore, Elgg can filter all blogs and group blog posts into four categories, when you click the **View all posts** link:

- **Personal blog posts**: These are blog posts made by you.
- **Community blog posts**: These are blog posts made by communities. We'll see how communities can post blogs in the next chapter.
- **Posts with comments**: These are all posts that have at least one comment.
- **Posts with no comments**: These are posts on which no users have commented.

Filtering blog posts into these categories gives users an immediate glance at the blog posts from the entire network. Posts with the most comments might be interesting and worth a look. You can also encourage new members who don't have any comments on their blog by adding some.

Preventing Spam

Allowing readers to comment on your blogs is a wonderful mechanism for online discussions. But spammers often use the commenting system to inject undesirable and inappropriate messages or advertisements.

Elgg has several tools that can help control and eliminate the various types of spam comments.

Who Can Comment?

Controlling access to the comments section on the blog is probably the easiest method of controlling spam.

By default, Elgg allows only users logged in to Elgg to comment on your posts. While this acts as a way to reduce the amount of spam, it doesn't stop registered users from spamming. Furthermore, several legitimate users might turn away from commenting to avoid being forced into registering before commenting.

Users can customize their individual spam settings. To change the setting:

1. Click the **Account settings** link.

2. Scroll down to the **Make comments public** section.

3. Depending on whether you want to allow non-registered members to comment or restrict to comments logged-in members, click **Yes** to make the comments public, otherwise choose **No**.

Make comments public

Set this to 'yes' if you would like anyone to be able to comment on your resources (by default only logged-in users can). Note that this may make you vulnerable to spam.

Public comments:

  ○ Yes ● No

Using Plug-ins

We've already discussed why spam is undesirable yet unavoidable in a public access system like a social network. In my experience, disallowing anonymous comments isn't a good idea. But it can be very dangerous without spam checking mechanisms. The whole point of a social network is to attract as many users as possible. But along with the sheep, come some wolves.

Elgg has two very useful plug-ins that will help us sort out the sheep from the wolves. The two systems use two very powerful and well respected tools and techniques to keep our network spam-free.

Implementing Captcha

Captcha is a popular comment verification technique, where users enter data displayed in an image. It's a challenge-response system, where the system takes on the user to verify if he is in fact a human being or a spamming script. A Captcha challenges the user to enter a random, distorted string of text.

The benefit of using Captcha is that it avoids the registration process. You can allow anonymous users to comment as long as they go through the Captcha process. It might add an extra step to commenting, but it's way better that restricting only registerted members to comment.

To use Captcha, download the plug-in (`http://elgg.org/mod/plugins/plugin.php?id=12`) and unzip it under Elgg's `mod/` directory. The plug-in requires the php-gd library, which will use the PHP language to convert random strings of text into images. Installing this library in your web server is covered in the Appendix that covers Elgg installation.

Once you have the Captcha directory in place under `mod/`, edit Elgg's `mod/blog/lib/weblogs_comments_add.php` file. Scroll down to around line 55-56, where it reads:

```
$run_result .= templates_draw(array(
                            'context' => 'databox1',
                            'name' => ' ',
                            'column1' => "<input type=\"submit\"
value=\"".__gettext("Add comment")."\" />"
                            )
                            );
```

Just above this section, enter the following two lines of code:

```
// Make room for entering the captcha data
$run_result .= run('weblog:comments:extrafield');
```

This code, as the comment reads, will display an additional text box where you can enter the Captcha image text. From now on, whenever anyone wants to comment on your blog, they'll have to enter the phrase displayed in the Captcha. If they enter it incorrectly, the plug-in will provide them with another image and ask them to try again with the message **Verification code incorrect. Please try again**.

Restricting to Anonymous Users

The plug-in as it stands now, will display a Captcha irrespective of whether the user is a registered member or an unregistered member. While this is quite a safe strategy, you can spare the registered members from having to verify themselves. It's fairly easy to restrict the Captcha to only non-registered members of the public.

Locate the plug-in's configuration file (mod/captcha/config.php). Scroll down to the 11th line, which reads:

```
define('captcha_anon_only', false); // set true to catch only
anonymous users
```

To restrict the plug-in to non-registered members, do as the comment says, and replace the false value with true. Now the line should read:

```
define('captcha_anon_only', true); // set true to catch only
anonymous users
```

Now when you log in and head back to a blog, to comment, you'll notice the Captcha image and the associated input box have both disappeared. Bookmark the direct URL of this blog entry and log out of the network. Use the bookmarked entry to go to the blog post. Now that you are an anonymous user of the network, you'll have to go through the plug-in before your comment can be added to the post.

Increasing the Vocabulary

I like the Captcha plug-in because not only is it very useful, but also its developer has made it very easy to configure and extend. Since the plug-in uses the php-gd library to create its own images, you can enter as many words to its repository as you want. What's more, you can even add to its list of fonts to display the Captcha in different styles.

Just open the plug-in's configuration file (mod/captcha/config.php) and scroll down to line 18. This section defines the plug-in's array of fonts. It reads:

```
// font list
$captcha_fonts = array(
  'adler.ttf',
  'ateliersans.ttf',
  'beatty.ttf',
  'jenkinsv.ttf',
  'wesley.ttf',
);
```

The fonts are bundled with the plug-in and are under its `inc/` directory (`mod/captcha/inc/`). You can delete fonts from this list if you want to. If you want to add a new font, first make sure it's in the `inc/` directory and then append it's name to this array.

Further down, on line 33 of the configuration file, you'll see the array of words the plug-in uses to turn into images. The section reads:

```
// choose words of 6 characters maximum
// should be 20 or more words
   $captcha_words = array(
            'abcd',
            'hola',
            'mundo',
            'spam',
            'blog',
            'elgg',
            );
```

You can add any number of words to this list. But make sure they follow the rule mentioned in the comments above and are a maximum of 6 characters.

But if you really want to mix it up, you can make the plug-in construct its own random words. Line 29 of the plug-in's configuration file, determines who controls the words to display—the user or the plug-in. By default, the plug-in uses the words in the array and the line reads:

```
// Set to true to take one word of the list,
// otherwise the code will be generated randomly
$captcha_use_wordlist = true;
```

To let the plug-in come up with random words, just change the `true` value to `false`. Now it should read:

```
$captcha_use_wordlist = false;
```

When the `use_wordlist` variable is turned off, the plug-in takes it upon itself to come up with a random mix of words and numbers.

Handling Improper Words

Not exactly spam, but some messages might contain inappropriate words. Abuse or derogatory slang take a discussion off-track and are an eyesore.

I personally enjoy Elgg's mechanism for automatically removing improper words from comments. It uses regular expressions which are a string of text that define a pattern, which can then match a wide set of strings. Regular expressions are what made the Perl programming language popular. They are easy to write yet very powerful.

Spam blocking

Main | Add users | Manage users | Banned users | Admin users | Manage flagged content | Spam control

Add regular expressions below, one per line, to block spam. For example, 'foo' will block all comments containing the word foo, (foo|bar) will block comments containing the word foo or bar.

Blank lines and lines starting with # will be ignored.

Regular expressions

```
#some common spammer's favorite keywords
enlargement
nicotine|viagra
```

Save

To enter patterns in Elgg, log in as the administrator user:

1. Click the **Administration** in the top panel.
2. From the administration section, click the **Spam control** link.
3. This opens a page that contains a huge text box, which lets you enter a set of regular expressions that will be matched against all comments. If a pattern matches those words, the comment will not be added to the post.

Your comment could not be posted. The system thought it was spam.

Downloading Blogs

Backing up data is always a good idea. If you love your ramblings, keep them backed up in case something breaks our over the network. Losing hours and hours of blogs over a delayed payment isn't worth it. Elgg has two simple tools to help you backup your blogs. And as with all things Elgg, you can use the data in several productive ways as well.

You'll find the two options from under the **Your Blog** area. The first option **Download blog as HTML** saves all your entries, as well as their tags in a simple HTML file. Since all the links in this file are preserved, you can even upload this and use it when your Elgg blog is inaccessible.

The **Download blog as RSS** option will save the file in RSS's XML format. The other benefit of saving the file in this format is that it can be used to import your blog in RSS readers.

Managing Resources

In computing terminology, a resource is usually something whose availability is limited. Managing those resources, like memory or disk space, means utilizing them appropriately. In Elgg terms though, resources are the means of accessing various information originating inside or outside the system.

Feeding Stuff

The best way to get access information from several sources is through feed aggregation. Feeds are special sources that serve users with frequently updated content. Distributors of the content put together a feed and allow visitors to subscribe to it. Collecting a bunch of feeds is known as aggregation.

As we discussed in the introductory chapter, using Elgg, you can not only subscribe to feeds but also make your own for others to subscribe to.

Creating Feeds

It's a good idea to create feeds to your blogs. This allows people to keep a tab on your blog and new posts, even if they forget your blog address. It also gives you a much broader audience than just the ones visiting your blog. Of course, it's also convenient to people who can browse through lots of blogs without actually visiting even one of them.

Since it's such a good idea, Elgg automatically creates feed for you! All your blog posts are already part of a feed. All the visitor has to do is copy-paste it into his favorite application. And if he's a member on your Elgg network, or is using one of the popular blogging feeds, the feeds can be subscribed to with a single mouse click!

What Feeds are Available?

Elgg creates a lot of feeds. Here's a list of all the feeds that it creates for the variety of content:

- Feeds for tags—all the tags in the tag could have their own custom feed to keep track of posts that use that particular tag.
- Feeds for search results—same as the one above but search results can also include tags that don't appear in the tag cloud.
- Feeds for web posts by a particular user.
- Feeds for a particular category by a particular user—this is more focused than the feed for all posts by a user. This feed only tracks posts that have been made under the category that's interesting to you and cuts out the rest of the posts.

> [RSS feed for weblog posts by Shashank Sharma in category 'technology']
>
> Syndication
>
> RSS feed for this tag

Inducting Feeds

As you can see, Elgg offers several feeds. Depending on your preference, you might want to subscribe to one or all of them. So how do you induct feeds of blogs you like?

It's actually very simple. Whenever you spot a feed in Elgg, you'll notice that they are all links. Clicking on them will take you to page that will describe the feed and let you subscribe to it.

This page has links to various popular aggregators, including Bloglines, My Yahoo, My MSN, Newsgator, and SoloSub. Just click on the appropriate service and the feed will be added to you account.

But if you are a member of the same Elgg network, you can simply click the big green button that reads **To add this feed to your resources page, click here** and you're done.

Adding Feeds from External Sources

Now that we know how to induct feeds from within the network, let's also take a look at adding feeds from external sites.

First locate a feed to subscribe to. Almost every news and blogging site, makes a feed that you can subscribe to. A typical feed URL ends with a .rss extension like this: http://www.linux.com/index.rss.

Log into your account and click the **Your Resources** link. On the main page of this section of the Elgg installation, you'll see a list of feeds you've subscribed to, if any. Also on the page is a text box. Simply copy-paste the link to the feed here and click the **Subscribe** button.

Adding Popular Feeds

There's one way to do something. And then there's the Elgg's way. So you are on a social network, and you have to hunt down and subscribe to your own feeds? As you would now have come to expect from Elgg, it has an alternative.

Elgg also keeps track of the most popular feeds on the network. Why is this useful? Since your Elgg network has members that share some common taste, there's a high probability that you'll like the feeds others have subscribed to as well. For example, if your Elgg network is about technology, or gadgets, you'll all be subscribing to popular technology news sites and blogs.

This is a list of the feeds with the most subscribers.

Last updated	Link to site	
June 08 2007, 21:30	Linux.com	View posts | Unsubscribe 3 Subscribers
June 08 2007, 20:01	OSNews	View posts | Unsubscribe 2 Subscribers
June 08 2007, 17:49	Shashank Sharma : Weblog	View posts | Subscribe 1 Subscribers

The **Popular Feeds** link under the **Your Resources** section, lists the most popular feeds on the network. The feeds are listed along with the numbers of subscribers, with the feed with the highest number of subscribers on top.

Feeds also have links to subscribing and unsubscribing a particular feed, depending of course, on whether you've subscribed to the feed or not. Before subscribing to a feed, you can also view the contents in that feed by clicking the **View posts** link.

Viewing the Feeds

Now that you have subscribed to a bunch of feeds, you need to check on them regularly.

Go to the **Your Resources** section, and from inside, click on the **View aggregator** link. This will show the contents of the feeds arranged in descending chronological order, with the most recent updates on the top.

News :: Feeds

Feeds | Publish to blog | View aggregator | Popular Feeds

June 08, 2007

KOffice 1.6.3 Released
The KOffice team has released KOffice 1.6.3. "This is the last maintenance release of the 1.6 series, containing mainly bug fixes. There are bug fixes for almost all of the components. See the complete changelog for the complete information."

via OSNews

It is can be LOLCODE time plz?
They're in ur Intarwebs, creating a programming language. The attack of the lolcats has spilled over to programming, with LOLCODE, a language based on the mangled grammar of lolcats. Pull up a buckit and I'll help wif ur understanding of LOLCODE.

via Linux.com

All items of the feed have a brief snippet of the piece and links to the detailed news item or the full blog post. Since the item can be from any of the feeds you've subscribed to, all items also include the name and link to the site they are from.

RSS Feed for Files

In addition to viewing files, visitors can also subscribe to feeds for your folders. This keeps them updated with new files that you might upload. Feeds are available for both individual file repositories as well as repositories hosted by a community.

Like with blogs, there are several types of feeds for files available. The most basic feed is the one that tracks all the contents of a user or a community. There's a link to this feed under the **Files** section in a user's profile page as well as the community's landing page.

Other types of feeds are available based on your search result. So, if you search for the term "linux", you'll be offered feeds for all files owned by a particular user that are in the category that you've searched, that is, "linux".

Podcasting with Elgg

Podcasting with Elgg is child's play. That is once you have a podcast—not that getting one is a tricky proposition! There is no dearth of tools that'll help you record and edit your own podcast. About.com has a page (`http://radio.about.com/od/podcastin1/a/aa030805a.htm`) that covers all aspects of podcasts blow-by-blow.

So once you have a podcast, how do you let the world know? You don't! Elgg will do it for you. All you have to do—and pay attention here—is upload your MP3 podcast to your file repository. Ok, so I was kidding about the pay attention part; there is just a one-step process to uploading and sharing podcasts. And this is that time of the chapter when I croon about Elgg's ease of use. Why else do you think this book is as small as it is?

The only thing you have to take care of is to make sure the podcasts are publically accessible. This is easily done by setting the **Access Restriction** on the podcasts to **Public**. It's a good idea to upload podcasts in a specific directory to keep them from mixing with the other files. If you upload podcasts to a directory—say it's named podcasts—make sure that the directory is publically accessible as well. Again, this can be done by setting the **Access Restriction** on the directory to **Public**.

Listening to Podcasts

Once you have uploaded a podcast, all your readers need to do is subscribe to your feed. This feed is different from your weblog feed. Your weblog feed only shared contents of your blog and can be subscribed to from under the weblog section. The weblog subscription feed is subscribed from a page that has a URL like http://geekybodhi.net/elgg/msharma/weblog/rss/.

The user feed has a much grander objective. It plugs all your activity. You can find the link to this feed under your user icon, the right-hand status bar. It has the following URL http://geekybodhi.net/elgg/msharma/rss/. Notice the difference?

Summary

Mayank Sharma : Activity

Activity for Mayank Sharma, hosted on My Elgg site.

- Blogs are a good thing.... >>

- Off to timbuktu >>

- Random titbits >>

   File: http://localhost/elgg9final/msharma/files/1/8/03032007.mp3 (audio/mp3)

- Episode Two >>

   File: http://localhost/elgg9final/msharma/files/1/7/Ep+2+More+Education.mp3 (audio/mp3)

- Random titbits >>

   File: http://localhost/elgg9final/msharma/files/1/6/02032007.mp3 (audio/mp3)

- Episode One >>

   File: http://localhost/elgg9final/msharma/files/1/5/Ep1+Education.mp3 (audio/mp3)

Once your listeners have subscribed to the feed from any podcast reader, they'll be automatically notified when a new episode is uploaded. As per the Elgg website, users have reported that Elgg podcasts work well with Odeo (http://odeo.com/), iTunes (http://www.apple.com/itunes/), and Juice (http://juicereceiver.sourceforge.net/).

So now you're hooked on to podcasting like bees take to honey. No longer satisfied by a solitary weekly podcast, you now in fact want to do one every day on a variety of topics. But not all your listeners may like to hear all the random ramblings. The good news is, they don't have to either.

If you separate the different podcasts with different tags, you can have a different feed for all your podcast series. For example, if you have a podcast series on education, while uploading the podcast episodes make sure they are tagged 'education'. Your personal ramblings can be tagged 'personal' and tag your sports podcast with 'sports'.

Now when you click on any keyword, Elgg will give you a link that says **RSS feed for files owned by Mayank Sharma in category 'education'**. The link points you to a RSS feed that looks something like **http://geekybodhi.net/elgg/msharma/files/ rss/education**. As you can see, it's a sub-set of your files tagged by the education keyword. Similarly, the feed for the personal tag will read: **http://geekybodhi.net/ elgg/msharma/files/rss/personal**.

Summary
Mayank Sharma : Files tagged with education
Files for Mayank Sharma, hosted on My Elgg site.

* Episode Two >>

    File: http://localhost/elgg9final/msharma/files/1/7/Ep+2+More+Education.mp3 (audio/mp3)

* Episode One >>

    File: http://localhost/elgg9final/msharma/files/1/5/Ep1+Education.mp3 (audio/mp3)

All you have to do now, is blog about the various podcasts, and point the readers/ listeners to the various feeds. Bravo, you're a podcasting star!

Blogging Podcasts

Since many people may have subscribed to your blog or may land up there instead of your podcast files, it makes sense to blog about your podcasts. Plus Elgg add its own nice little touch when you blog podcasts, which might tempt you to blog all your podcasts.

Adding a podcast to a post isn't any different from adding any other file. As described earlier in this chapter, you'll have to insert the unique number of a file from your repository within a pair of curly braces ({{ }}). Check out the image for a sample post with a link to the podcast.

Post title:

Education Series podcast

Add External video   Add File

Post body:

B *I* U | ABC ≡ ≡ ≡ ≡ ≣ ≣ ⚡ ↺ ↻ ⮑ ⮑ HTML 🌳 ▾ ☺

🖃 ¶ 🔍 🔧

I have started a weekly podcast show on Education. If you are interested in using electronic tools to teach (and learn), please tune in every Wednesday.

In the first show I talk about iTALC, the open source didactical tool. Hear it here :)

{{file:5}}

And subscibe to the feed here: http://geekybodhi.net/elgg/msharma/files/rss/

Path:

Doesn't seem all that different from any other post, correct? But once published, the post looks like the image below:

Education Series podcast

I have started a weekly podcast show on Education. If you are interested in using electronic tools to teach (and learn), please tune in every Wednesday.

In the first show I talk about iTALC, the open source didactical tool. Hear it here :)

◄◄ ►■ ►► HIDEOUT XSPF MUSIC PLAYER - BY FABRICIO ZUARDI ...ıllll

And subscibe to the feed here: http://geekybodhi.net/elgg/msharma/files/rss/

Keywords: education, italc, podcast

As you can see, Elgg's wrapped a music player around your podcast. Your listeners can listen to the podcast as it streams live from your website, without downloading it, thanks to the embedded music player. Does Elgg ooze coolness or what?

Summary

In this chapter, we've looked at the most important aspect of any website—creating content. We've used Elgg's blogging system to post blog entries. More importantly, we've also covered the various Elgg mechanisms for minimizing abuse of the system. In case the system is abused, we've seen how to deal with the off-topic content.

Also in this chapter, we've understood Elgg's comprehensive commenting system. To ensure spam comments don't interfere in the discussions, we've learnt how to use Elgg's spam control tools.

Once we are done creating content, the chapter explains sharing the content through feeds. Elgg provides us with various feeds that we can feed with external visitors or users of the same Elgg network. We've looked at using Elgg's social networking capabilities to find and subscribe to the most popular and relevant feeds subscribed to by the users on the network.

We've also covered how Elgg handles multimedia content, both internal and external. We've learnt to use different types of content, irrespective of their point of origin. Video files, PDF's, images, and podcasts, with Elgg you can share them all.

5
Communities and Files

Ah! Take a breather. Sit back and enjoy seeing your network grow! See members come and join the network, populate their profiles, and make connections with others. Watch them create information by blogging, and bring more information into the network through feeds. Wonderful!

But that's not all! Elgg packs in another powerful tool that'll help members of your social network interact better. Using Elgg, members can form virtual communities around a broad subset of the social network. Members have common interests and goals.

Virtual communities are also known as online communities, because its members interact via the Internet. Being online, also lets them interact across time and geographical boundaries. There are different methods of contributing in a virtual community. For example, a member might write blog entries or message boards while another member may add comments. Elgg provides several means of contributing and managing an online community.

Creating Communities

Like everything in Elgg, creating a community is a walk in the park. But before creating a community, search for similar communities. If a community on your topic exists, creating a duplicate community will hamper growth of both yours, and the existing community.

Search for Existing Communities

Searching for communities isn't any different from searching for anything else in Elgg. You use the same search text box on the top of the page. You can choose to let Elgg search all types of contents for the terms or just restrict it to searching communities. For the latter, instead of **--all--** option select the **Communities** option.

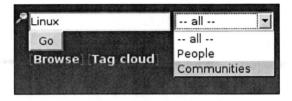

In the results page, if there are communities matching your search term, they'll be listed under the **Matching users and communities:** section.

Matching users and communities:

Linux Lovers

Once you are sure that a community on your topic doesn't exist, you can steam ahead and start your very own community.

Hatching a Community

Like every resource on Elgg, and this is true generally as well, a community needs a name. Internally, though, Elgg treats a community like any other member on the network. This has its benefits, as we'll discuss shortly.

So, to create a community, head over to the **Your Network** area after logging in. We've been into this area before to manage our contacts in the network and make new friends.

Navigate to the **Owned Communities** link in this section. When you click the link, Elgg will list the communities you own. Because you don't own any, it'll suggest to create one. Take up its order and fill in the two simple and straightforward details.

> **Community Name**: The name of the community as it'll appear to others.
>
> **Username for Community**: Like I just mentioned, a community is like any other member, so it needs to have a username as well.

```
Create a new community

Community name:

Linux Admins


Username for community:

commadmin


Create
```

That's it. Click the **Create** button, and the community is live. Since you created the community, you are automatically added as a member.

Your community was created and you were added as its first member.

Grooming the Community

Like I said, creating a community is pretty simple. But the community we just created looks very "raw". It's a good idea to work on it a little and make it more presentable before inviting members.

You'll be surprised how seriously Elgg treats a community like any other member. In addition to the community getting its own username, it also gets a profile, just like you do!

But why does a community need a profile? Well, just like you need one to describe yourself, your community needs one to present itself to other members. A community's profile does the same job as your own profile. Visitors to the community read through its profile to decide whether it interests them or not.

So let's go ahead and give our community a personality.

Community Profile

Click on the community to edit it. When you do, you're flown to an area from where you can hack various details about the community.

To fill up the community's profile, click the **Edit this profile** link. As you can see, it doesn't appear to be much different from the profile page we used to fill up our own profile. Even the options and access control don't seem to be any different.

```
Linux Admins :: Edit profile                                   Profile Owner

Edit this profile | Community site picture | Edit community details | View membership requests

This screen allows you to edit your profile. Blank fields will not show up on your profile screen in any view; you      Linux Admins
can change the access level for each piece of information in order to prevent it from falling into the wrong            RSS | Tags | Resources
hands. For example, we strongly recommend you keep your address to yourself or a few trusted parties.

 Basic details   Location   Contact   Employment   Education                          Click here to leave this
                                                                                      community.
Introduction
A short introduction to this community.                                               Blog

This community is for Linux administrators. Here we share tips and shortcuts to help us      Community blog ( RSS)
with our day-to-day tasks. If you are a new Linux user interested in administrating your
Linux box, this community might not be a good option. We use terms that might sound greek    Weblog Archive
to non admins. While we'd love to help out new users, this community isn't the place to
look for newbie handholding. There are plenty of communities for new Linux users on the      Friends blog
network.
                                                                                      Files

                                                                                         File Storage (0 files)

                                                                                         ( RSS)

Access Restriction:                                                                   Members
Public                                                                                   News
Brief description
For use in your sidebar profile.                                                         Members

A community for Linux administrations to share tips and shortcuts.

Access Restriction:
Public
```

Fill in the details that are relevant to the community and leave the rest. I generally fill in an introduction to the community and a brief description for the side bar and make them public for everyone to see.

 You can also use the Interests and Likes field to add keywords that describe the community.

Community Picture

Once you have set up the profile, you should put up a picture that identifies your profile. The procedure for uploading a picture to use with the community is the same as uploading your own picture.

Click on the community to enter its editing side. Once there, click the **Community site picture** link. From the **Picture to upload** section, click the **Browse** button and locate the file you want to use as the community's icon. Add an optional description for the icon in the text box under the **Icon description** section. Finally, from the pull-down menu under the **Make this the default icon** option, choose **Yes**. To upload the image and use it as an icon, click the **Upload new icon** button.

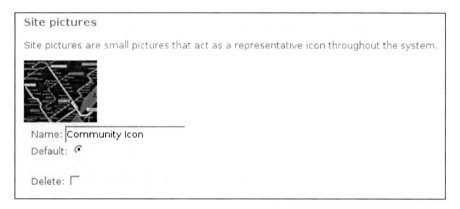

Icons are resized to Elgg's 100 pixel x 100 pixel resolution. Some larger images might lose clarity at this resolution. After an icon has been uploaded, Elgg resizes it and in the following screen, you can preview the icon as it will appear on the site. If you don't like the icon, select the **Delete** check-box to delete the icon and upload again. If everything's hunky dory, click the **Save** button to use it as the community's default icon.

Announcing the Community

Inviting users to join the community is a natural extension to creating the community. Unfortunately, the stable version of Elgg, available at the time of writing this book (version 0.8), doesn't have any process for announcing the community to potential members.

However, in the latest release candidate of Elgg 0.9 (Elgg 0.9rc1), community owners can search for people by their username or real name and then invite them to join their community.

Joining the Community

So you've made noise about your community and depending on how interested people are about the topic, members will start trickling in. The community will also start appearing in relevant searches.

On the community's landing page, visitors will see a description about the community and any other detail we've entered in the profile. If they are enticed, joining the community is pretty easy. All they need to do is find the link in the right-hand-side-bar that reads **Click here to join this community** and click it. A window will pop-up confirming their action.

After a user has joined the community, it'll be listed under his network in the communities section.

Membership Restriction

By default, Elgg allows everyone to join your community. Depending on what sort of community you're running, you might want to take charge of the registration process.

Elgg lets you moderate membership to your community. This is similar in nature and function to moderating friendship requests. Think of members as friends of the community.

You can choose from the three preset moderation levels:

No moderation: anyone can join the community.

Moderation: memberships must be approved by you.

Private: nobody can join this community.

To change the moderation level, click the community. From the community administration bar, click the **Edit community details** link. Here, scroll down to the **Membership restriction** section and from the drop down list, choose the option that suits you and click the **Save** button at the bottom to apply the changes.

Handling Membership Requests

Let's suppose you've decided to moderate members' joining the community. Now when members land on your community's main page, the **Click here to join this community** link has been replaced by **Click here to apply to join this community** link.

Now when members click on the link, they are added to your moderation queue. You, as the administrator of the community, need to approve or reject their membership.

Membership of Linux Admins needs to be approved. Your request has been added to the list.

All membership requests are logged for community owners. To see a list of requests, go to your community and from the community administration bar click the **View membership requests** link.

To help you decide whether a member is "worthy" of joining your community, Elgg gives you several details about the member. In addition to the name and picture of the member requesting access, you get his brief profile, link to his complete profile, and his blog.

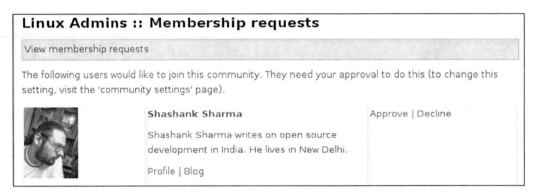

Depending on your yardstick for evaluating members, you can either accept or decline the request. If you click on the **Decline** link, Elgg will not add the member to your community and also remove him from the list of people requesting access. On the other hand, if you do decide to admit the member and click on the **Accept** link, the member is added to your community.

Leaving the Community

For whatever reason, if a user decides to leave your community, he can easily do so. After joining the community, the link that invites members of the network to join the community, changes to **Click here to leave this community**. To leave the community, click the link to delist from the community.

Click here to leave this community.

Unlike the mob, you don't need approval for leaving the community. All users in a community can leave on their own free will, so there's no moderation option to approve delisting.

Community Ownership

By default, Elgg makes the user who has created the community its administrator or owner. Owning a community means you have to look after it, and administer its operations. This includes moderating membership requests, controlling the look and feel of the community, and keeping it active while ensuring discussions don't go off topic.

This isn't an easy job! Maybe after a while you want to hand over administration to another loyal, long-time, and active member. This is easily done.

From your community's administration bar, click the **Edit community details** link and scroll down to the **Community ownership** section. Under this section, in the text box associated with the **Community owner** option, Elgg lists the username of the owner of the community. Currently, it should display your user name.

As the **Community owner** option states, the text box cannot be empty. Before replacing your username with another username, make sure the username is valid and in use. After entering the username of the member you want to transfer control to, press the **Save** button at the bottom of the page. Elgg confirms that control has been transferred to another member.

Community ownership transferred to shashanks.

Two things happen as soon as you hand over control. Firstly, the community you've transferred disappears from your list of **Owned Communities**. You are relegated to a normal user of the community. Secondly, the community now has a new owner—the member who has been made the new administrator. He also gets the community administration bar with links to control and edit the community.

Using the Community

Till now, we've been discussing how to control and manage a community on Elgg. Now, let's shift our attention to using the community for creating content. Elgg bundles two very powerful and flexible content generation tools for communities—blogs and forums. Let's look at them closely.

Community Blog

On the community's main page, the right-side vertical panel has a section dedicated to blogs. The **Blog** section has links to the community's blog, its RSS feed, the weblog's archive, and also a collection of posts from the community's friend's blog.

Blog
Community blog (RSS)
Weblog Archive
Friends blog

Let's tackle these one by one. A Community's blog is much like a normal blog. But instead of just one blogger, all members of the community can blog on the community's blog. To post a new entry, members need to click the **Community blog** link in the side bar. From the blogging section, they need to click the **Post a new entry** link. This opens Elgg's WYSIWYG blogging interface, similar to the interface they get for their own respective blogs.

To view the content of the community's blog, click the **View blog** link from the blogging section of the community. The display is similar to your own personal blog. But of course, instead of your own blog, you have several other bloggers on the same page as you.

Elgg is also smart enough to distinguish blog posts that you make on your personal blog or in some community. While identifying the poster who has made a particular blog post, Elgg appends the name of the community as well. For example, if I make a blog post entry in a community called Linux Admins, Elgg will credit the post to **Mayank Sharma @ Linux Admins**.

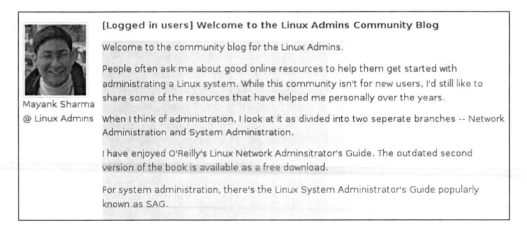

Mayank Sharma
@ Linux Admins

[Logged in users] Welcome to the Linux Admins Community Blog

Welcome to the community blog for the Linux Admins.

People often ask me about good online resources to help them get started with administrating a Linux system. While this community isn't for new users, I'd still like to share some of the resources that have helped me personally over the years.

When I think of administration, I look at it as divided into two seperate branches -- Network Administration and System Administration.

I have enjoyed O'Reilly's Linux Network Adminsitrator's Guide. The outdated second version of the book is available as a free download.

For system administration, there's the Linux System Administrator's Guide popularly known as SAG.

Remember that all members of a community are its friends. The **Friends' blog** link shows blog posts made by all members either in the community blog or in their personal blogs. This is where ear-marking community blog posts come in handy. You can use the **View all posts** link to filter blog posts that appear in your personal blog ad that you've made in a community blog.

Removing Improper Posts

Because all users can create blog posts in a community blog, the chances of abuse are higher. A community blog owner has to be on his toes to keep the posts clean and healthy. The power to delete or edit posts lie with either the user who has created the blog post or the owner/administrator of the community.

Elgg treats the administrator of the community as the owner of all pieces of content, so removing/editing posts from the community blog is similar to removing them from their own blog. Head over to the community and navigate to the offending post. There you'll find control to edit and/or delete the post. Make your pick!

Moderating Communities

As Elgg allows all members to create and own communities, some users might create communities that are against your policy. Editing or removing a few posts to keep a community clean is one thing, but what if the entire community is "dirty"?

Fear not! Once you are aware of such a community, you can easily get rid of it. But Elgg only allows owners of the communities to delete them. And if the community is corrupt, it's only because their owners are as well. So, you'll first have to snatch control from the owners by editing the community details as covered in the "Community Ownership" section previously.

Once you own the community, just head over to **Your Network | Owned communities**. Elgg will list all the communities you own including the offensive one, along with a link to **Delete community**. Use it!

Other Community Administration

All throughout this chapter, we've covered various aspects of setting up and controlling communities. But still, there are some other simple yet important community administration options on offer.

The options can all be modified by the community administrator. They can be accessed from the community administration section by clicking the **Edit community details** link:

Community: This section handles the name of the community. There can be various reasons why you want to change the name of the community. Maybe what you entered while setting up the community doesn't describe the community too well. Maybe the community has evolved and grown to encompass more details or become more specialized. Whatever the reason, if you want to change the name of the community, just replace the current name in the text box with the new one and you're done.

Change your community name
This name will be displayed throughout the system.

Community name

Linux "Network" Admins

Language: if you're running a localized network, you can change the language of the community as well. Just select from one of the supported languages from the drop down box in the **Language selection** section. Choices available include English, German, Spanish, Basque, French, Hungarian, Icelandic, Italian, Korean, Lithuanian, Norwegian, Dutch, Portuguese, Russian, Swedish, and Chinese.

Language selection:

Choose your preferred language for this site. The following languages are available on this system:

Language selection:

English/United Kingdom ▾

default
German
English/United Kingdom
Spanish
Basque
French
Hungarian
Icelandic
Italian
Korean
Lithuanian
Norwegian Bokmål
Dutch
Portuguese/Brazil
Russian
Swedish
Chinese/China

Quotas: This field is used to control the size of files that members of a community can upload. The figure is specified in bytes. By default, it's set to 1000000000 bytes, which is equal to almost 954 MB. Use Google Calculator (`http://www.google.co.in/intl/en/help/features.html#calculator`) to bring this figure down to a reasonable amount of space, like 20 MB or 20971520 bytes. Replace the existing size with the new size in the space provided.

```
Change file quota (in bytes):

New file quota:

20971520
```

WYSIWYG Editor: If you want to save on bandwidth at the risk of making blog posts a little inconvenient to new users, you can turn off the WYSIWYG editor. Just select to disable the visual editor. Also, remember these settings are overruled by the visual editor settings in the user's **Account settings** section.

```
Add a new post

Post title:

WYSIWYG editor switched off

Post body:

To save bandwidth we've switched off the visual editor. You'll have to use to HTML tags to
make text <b>bold</b> and such. |
```

Community Forum

Online forums are a great medium for interacting with other members. They open lines of communication between members that follow a particular thread that is basically an online version of a chain of thought. Over the years, forums have established themselves as the best means to interact online.

Unfortunately, Elgg doesn't have a forum. But thanks to its malleable nature, you can use a community's blog as a forum! Once installed, the forum plug-in is designed to turn a community's blog into a forum board. The best part is that this "conversion" is purely visual. On the inside, things are done the same and you don't have to learn a new mechanism of posting to the community forum.

To install the plug-in, just download it [http://elgg.org/mod/plugins/plugin. php?id=6] and unzip in Elgg's mod/ directory. You'll then have to add the following lines to the end of your Elgg's .htaccess file:

```
##
#FOR FORUM PLUGIN
##
RewriteRule ^([A-Za-z0-9]+)\/forum\/?$ mod/forum/forum.php?weblog=$1
RewriteRule ^([A-Za-z0-9]+)\/forum\/skip=([0-9]+)$ mod/forum/forum.
php?weblog=$1&weblog_offset=$2
RewriteRule ^[A-Za-z0-9]+\/forum\/([0-9]+)(\.html)?$ mod/forum/forum_
view_thread.php?post=$1
```

Then log in as the administrator user (by default, this is the user 'news'), which will update the database to store some forum-related information. Optionally, you can also edit the plug-in's configuration file (<elgg-install-directory>/mod/forum/ config.php), which looks like this:

```
//SETUP THE FORUM DEFAULT FOR YOUR ELGG SYSTEM
//0=All community blogs become forum UNLESS the community owner sets a
flag to go back to being a community blog
//1=All community blogs remain community blogs UNLESS the community
owner sets a flag to turn them into a forum
//this flag is set in the "Edit Community details" area
$forum_default = 0;
//SETUP THE FORUM SORTING ATTRIBUTES FOR YOUR ELGG SYSTEM
//0=Forum discussions are sorted by the date of the original post
(newest thread goes at top)
//1=Forum discussions are sorted by the "last updated" attribute
of the thread so that active   discussions rise to the top of the
forum...
//NOTE: THIS REQUIRES THE ADDITION OF A NEW FIELD IN THE weblog_posts
table ("last_updated  int(11)      NULL ")
//THIS SHOULD HAPPEN AUTOMATICALLY WHEN YOU LOG IN AS "NEWS" after
installing this plugin
//NOTE: YOU WON'T SEE ANY EFFECT OF THIS CHANGE UNTIL A THREAD IS
UPDATED (weblog_post is edited, or a comment added/deleted)
$forum_sort = 1;
```

That's it. Now visit a community blog and you'll notice a link in the top navigation bar that reads **View as Forum**. Click on it to convert your blog into a forum board!

Linux "Network" Admins :: Blog

| Post a new entry | View blog | Archive | Friends' blogs | View all posts | Manage blog categories | View as Forum

You'll notice how the blog suddenly transforms into a forum board. All the blog posts are listed as discussions. Comments on the blog post now form the discussion thread of the forum topic. If you want to add a new thread, you can use the **Add New Item** link which will take you to the community's **Add a new post** page. This basically means that adding a new forum thread isn't any different from adding a new blog post.

Linux "Network" Admins :: Forum

| | Add New Item | View as Blog

DISCUSSION TOPIC	STARTED BY	COMMENTS
cron for backup	Mayank Sharma	0
Automatically saving configuration files	Mayank Sharma	2

Add New Item...

Handling Files

Files play an important part of our Elgg social network. As we've seen in previous sections and chapters, we can embed files in blog posts or share them with other members. Of course, we can also control the amount of space allotted to individual users and communities for uploading files.

Elgg has special mechanisms for dealing with different formats of files. It also has a very friendly method for organizing stored files in folders. Elgg stores data hierarchically in folders. Starting with the Root folder, a folder can have several files or several folders, which can again have files or more folders and so on.

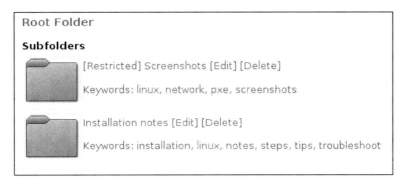

Creating Folders

Files are managed through the **Your Files** section of Elgg. When you first enter that section, Elgg will inform you that the Root folder is empty. It also presents you with a form to upload files or create new folders.

The folder creation form has 4 fields:

- **Name**: The name of the folder.
- **Folder Type**: Elgg has two types of folders, one for storing images (Photo Gallery) and the other for storing all other types of files (Default File Folder). We'll discuss them in detail as we upload files in them.
- **Access Restriction**: By now, you should be absolutely clear what this is. You can restrict access to the file to Elgg's pre-defined groups or your custom groups of friends or even communities.
- **Keywords**: Just like in blogs, keywords make your files more searchable if that's what you want. If these folders will hold private files, you can avoid listing keywords.

To create a folder, enter the name and keywords that describe the type of content inside the folder. You also have to choose the type of folder. By default, Elgg creates folders to hold documents. While you can store images in these folders as well, it's better to use the "Photo gallery" option when creating folders that'll hold images. Finally, specify who you want to share this folder with by selecting the appropriate user group from the pull-down menu.

Create a new folder

To create a new folder, enter its name:	Screenshots
Folder type:	Photo gallery ▼
Access restrictions:	Community: Linux "Network" Admins ▼
Keywords (comma separated):	linux, network, screenshots, pxe

Create

Uploading Files

The procedure for uploading files is the same regardless of the type of folder you're uploading to. Before you can upload files, make sure you are inside the correct folder. By default, you are at the Root folder. To move into one of the folders we've created, simply click on the name of the folder, which is in reality a hyperlink.

All the files you upload here will be uploaded into the current folder.

The file upload form has 5 fields:

- **File to upload**: The path to the file you want to upload.
- **File title**: Title of the file to help users identify it.
- **File description**: A description of the contents of the file.
- **Access restriction**: Controls the group of people who can view the file.
- **Keywords**: To make your file more searchable and show up in the tag cloud.

To upload a file, move into the folder that you want to keep the file under. Then click on the **Browse** button to locate the file on your computer. Add a title and description to it. Choose the group that can access the file and add relevant keywords.

Upload a file

Used space: 0 Mb.

File to upload: /home/bodhi/book.pdf   Browse...

File title: Installation Hand book

File Description: This is small (free) ebook that covers Linux installation.

Access restrictions: Community: Linux "Network" Admins ▾

Keywords (comma separated): linux, installation, ebook, book, newbie, install

☑ By checking this box, you are asserting that you have the legal right to share this file, and that you understand you are sharing it with other users of the system.

Upload

Right to Share

One thing you'd have noticed while uploading files is a check box at the bottom. The check box reads **By checking this box, you are asserting that you have the legal right to share this file, and that you understand you are sharing it with other users of the system**.

This is quite self explanatory. As an administrator, you wouldn't want people to misuse the ability of upload files by sharing copyrighted files.

Adding Files to a Community Repository

The process of uploading files in a community repository is similar to uploading them in your personal storage space. The only difference is that all members of a community can upload files to a community's file repository.

To upload a file to a community, a member needs to go to the community landing page. Here he should look for the "Files" section in the right-hand vertical menu. From this menu click the "File Storage" link to be flown to the community's file management screen. This is similar to the one you have for your own files. So you can create folders and files in the same hierarchical format as you can with your own file repository.

> The stable version of Elgg available at the time of writing this book, doesn't allow multiple files to be uploaded at one go. But the latest available release candidate of the next version (Elgg-0.9rc1) allows up to 5 files to be uploaded at one go. The procedure isn't different from the one covered in this book.

Send Messages

While Elgg has several methods of interaction, like communities and blogs, which users can use to communicate with each other, there isn't a direct method of communication. Most of the communication is handled by Elgg on behalf of the users. For example, when users on your network want to connect online, depending on their connection preferences, Elgg will send a friend request from one user to the other.

While this system works, there are several reasons why you'd like to communicate with other users. As an administrator, it'll help you carry out your duties better. For example, you can warn users disobeying community rules or hosting material on their blogs in violation of the network policy.

A direct communication system will also help establish another line of communication between members on your network. Users can use the system to send a message to the owner of a community or to each other.

Since Elgg lacks an in-built direct communication system, you'll have to rely on the messages plug-in. This plug-in is very easy to install. Just grab it [http://elgg.org/mod/plugins/plugin.php?id=18] and uncompress under Elgg's mod/ directory. Follow this up by pasting the following ReWrite rules to your .htaccess file:

```
##
# For the Messages plugin
##
RewriteRule ^([A-Za-z0-9]+)\/messages/$ mod/messages/index.
php?profile_name=$1
RewriteRule ^([A-Za-z0-9]+)\/messages\/msg_offset/([0-9]+)$ mod/
messages/index.php?profile_name=$1&msg_offset=$2
RewriteRule ^([A-Za-z0-9]+)\/messages\/sent$ mod/messages/index.
php?profile_name=$1&sent=1
RewriteRule ^([A-Za-z0-9]+)\/messages\/sent\/msg_offset/([0-9]+)$ mod/
messages/index.php?profile_name=$1&sent=1&msg_offset=$2
RewriteRule ^([A-Za-z0-9]+)\/messages\/compose$ mod/messages/compose.
php?profile_name=$1
RewriteRule ^([A-Za-z0-9]+)\/messages\/view\/([0-9]+)\/([0-1])$ mod/
messages/view.php?profile_name=$1&message=$2&sent=$3
```

Now, just log in to your network as the administrator user and watch the plug-in update Elgg's database to incorporate the information that will be transferred via the message plug-in. Once it's done, you'll notice a new addition to the navigation bar at the top of your screen that reads **Your Messages (0)**.

Click on the link to enter your message control area. The interface is pretty simple and straightforward. The main screen lists the messages you have received. The messages can be notifications of comments on your blog post or your profile (via the comment wall plug-in) from anonymous users, or messages sent by other users to you directory or to the admin of the communities you administrate.

When you click on a message you have the option to reply to it or delete it. You can also "Compose" new messages and send them to the communities you're subscribed to, or to your friends on the network. Whether you compose and send messages or reply to received messages, all sent messages are accessible via the **Sent Messages** link.

In addition to an additional line of communication between friends, another benefit of the messages plug-in is that it allows users to get to know each other better even before they join as friends on the network. As users explore your network, move through communities, discover other users, they'll notice a **Send Message** link at every profile (of an individual or a community) they run into. They can ask questions regarding the community to the administrator before joining or touch base with new users before adding them to their friends list.

Sharing Bookmarks

Social bookmarking isn't a new concept. Keeping your bookmarks online means they'll be accessible to you from any computer. But it's also a great way to share your resources with your online friends.

The bookmark plug-in adds the capability of sharing and storing bookmarks in Elgg. Just grab the plug-in [http://elgg.org/mod/plugins/plugin.php?id=30], unzip it and place its' _bookmarks folder under Elgg's main directory. The mod/bookmarks folder goes inside Elgg's mod/ folder and the units/bookmarks folder sits in the units folder under your Elgg installation.

Finally, add the following lines to your .htaccess file:

```
##
#For the Bookmarks plugin
##
RewriteRule ^([A-Za-z0-9]+)\/bookmarks\/?$ _bookmarks/subscriptions.
php?profile_name=$1
RewriteRule ^([A-Za-z0-9]+)\/bookmarks\/([0-9]+)\/?$ _bookmarks/
subscriptions.php?profile_name=$1&bookmark_id=$2
RewriteRule ^([A-Za-z0-9]+)\/bookmarks\/all\/?$ _bookmarks/index.
php?profile_name=$1
ReWriteRule ^([A-Za-z0-9]+)\/bookmarks\/all\/skip=([0-9]+)$ _
bookmarks/index.php?profile_name=$1&bookmark_offset=$2
RewriteRule ^[A-Za-z0-9]+\/bookmarks\/([0-9]+)\.html$ _bookmarks/view_
post.php?post=$1
```

```
RewriteRule ^[A-Za-z0-9]+\/bookmarks\/([0-9]+)\.html.([0-9]+)$ _
bookmarks/view_post.php?post=$1&commentpage=$2
RewriteRule ^([A-Za-z0-9]+)\/bookmarks\/tags\/?$ _bookmarks/tags.
php?profile_name=$1
RewriteRule ^([A-Za-z0-9]+)\/bookmarks\/rss\/(.+)\/?$ _bookmarks/rss2.
php?bookmark_name=$1&tag=$2&modifier=is
RewriteRule ^bookmarks\/popular$ _bookmarks/popular.php
RewriteRule ^bookmarks\/popular\/skip/([0-9]+)$ _bookmarks/popular.
php?skip=$1
```

When you head over to your Elgg network and log in as the administrator, the plug-in will update the database and notify you. You'll also notice an additional **Your Bookmarks** link in the navigation bar at the top of your screen.

From the **Bookmarks** section you can save new bookmarks or import existing bookmarks from a bookmarks file, like that created by the Firefox browser. You can also export bookmarks out of Elgg for either inserting them into Internet Explorer, or Mozilla's Firefox browser. The plug-in will also spill out bookmarks in XBEL (XML Bookmark Exchange Language) format that is used by social bookmarking networks like Del.icio.us and browsers like Galeon and Konqueror.

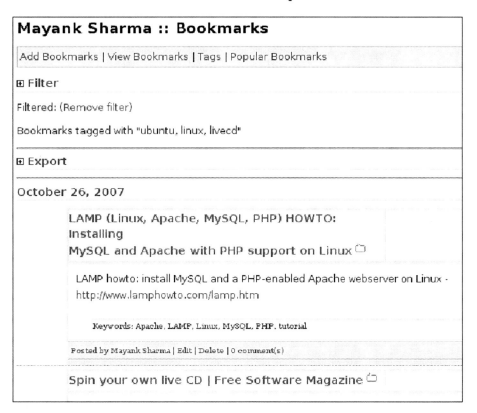

Just like other resources on Elgg, for example weblog posts, users can add tags to their bookmarks, comment on them, and set access restrictions. Users can also find popular bookmarks and look for the most used tags. The system also keeps an eye on the bookmark to make sure it doesn't return any errors. When it does, you can easily remove that bookmark.

Using Files

So now that you have a bunch of files up, it's time we discuss how they can be used. Also, remember all your files and even communities are added to your profile. So when a user visits your profile now, he'll notice all your owned communities and files repository in the right-side vertical menu.

Files

File Storage (5 files)

(RSS)

Owned communities

Linux Lovers

Linux "Network" Admins

Viewing Files

Visitors to your profile have several ways of reaching your file repository. They can either get to them through your profile, or by finding them using the search box or tag cloud.

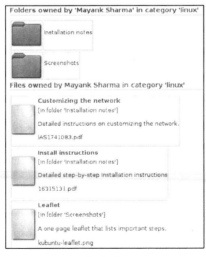

To view the files, visitors can click on the file and view them from this page itself. But if the file they want to view is an image file in a folder of type `Photo gallery`, then the best way to view the file is to change into the parent folder.

As I mentioned earlier, a `Photo gallery` folder is a special type of folder for storing and displaying files of images. When inside the folder, visitors get thumbnail previews of the images. On clicking, the images are displayed in a special JavaScript gallery. The background fades in to reveal the image in the foreground.

RSS Feed for Files

In addition to viewing files, visitors can also subscribe to feeds of your folders. This keeps them updated with new files that you might upload. Feeds are available for both individual file repositories as well as repositories hosted by a community.

As with blogs, there are several types of feeds for files available. The most basic feed is the one that tracks all the contents of a user or a community. There's a link to this feed under the **Files** section in a user's profile page as well as the community's landing page.

Other types of feeds are available based on your search result. So if you search for the term "Linux" you'll be offered feeds for all files owned by a particular user that are in the category that you've searched, that is, "Linux".

Moving and Deleting Files/Folders

You can easily move files from one folder to another or delete them altogether. If you are the owner of the files or folders, you'll notice two links next to them — **[Edit]** and **[Delete]**.

If you click the edit link of a file, you'll be able to modify any of its five parameters — title, description, access restriction, keywords, and the folder they reside in. If you want to move the file to another folder, select the appropriate folder. Or if you want to modify its description, type in a new one in the space provided. Once you are done making the changes, click on the **Save** button and Elgg will apply the changes.

Edit Leaflet

File title:	Leaflet
File description:	A single page leaflet that covers Kubuntu installation.
Access restrictions:	Logged in users
File folder:	Root
	Root
	> Screenshots
Keywords (comma separated):	> Installation notes kubuntu, leaflet

Save

Similarly, if you click the edit link of a folder, you can change any of its five parameters as well — folder name, access restriction, keywords, type of folder, and parent folder. Once you have made the changes, click the **Save** button to apply them.

Deleting files or folders is pretty simple and straightforward. Just hit the delete button next to the file or the folder you want to remove.

Remember that when you delete a folder, Elgg only removes the folder and moves the files or folders under it to the parent folder of the folder being deleted. For example, suppose you have a folder called Podcasts under the Root folder. The Podcast folder holds several .OGG music files. Now, if you remove the Podcast folder, it will be deleted, but Elgg will move all the .OGG files to the Root folder.

Embedding Files in Blogs

While we were discussing blogging in Chapter 4, I mentioned that you could embed files from your file repository in your posts? Now that we have a file repository, let's go back to our blog and use one of the files in our post.

When you head over to the blogging section to post a new entry, scroll down to the pull-down menu. It lists all your folders and files. Simply select the file you want to embed and click on the **Add** button. This will append a simple piece of code into your blog post's body. The code is actually a number enclosed in curly braces: {{file:5}}.

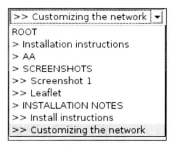

What Does the Number Mean?

Elgg assigns a unique number to each file and folder. You can view the number by hovering over a file in the **Your Files** section. The number will appear in the status bar of the browser.

So for example if you see something like **http://localhost/elgg/news/files/6/5/ lAS1741083.pdf**, this means the file **lAS1741083.pdf** is available from the user whose username is **news**. The file has the number 5 and is inside a folder with the number 6.

Removing Inappropriate Files/Folders

Like we've discussed earlier, unmoderated content creation is always abused. Elgg lets administrators of the network control any file or folder. You can delete any offending file or folder. As administrators, you'll always see the **[Edit]** and **[Delete]** links next to folders and files even if you don't own them.

Furthermore, a malicious file or folder will have a tough time surviving under the community. This is because all community members are equal owners of the file. They wouldn't require your administrative powers to get rid of offending material. They can do so themselves.

Summary

This is one of the most important chapters of the book because it deals with the most basic social networking technique-interaction betwen users. Creating communities and sharing thoughts are two very important functions of a network.

A community in Elgg lets you socialize with other members either through a blog or through a forum. Implementation-wise, Elgg treats a community like any other member. This is beneficial because you get similar looking screens for posting blogs and other controls like you do in your user account. In a community blog, all members can make blog posts. The only difference between posts in your personal blog and in that of a community is that community posts are around the topic of the community.

Of course, learning to manage these tools takes some time. Since they allow unmoderated content to be generated, your role as an administrator becomes all the more important. After reading the chapter, you should be fully equipped with the skills to create and manage a powerful social network.

6
Customizing Elgg

Setting up Elgg is all about customizing. In the previous chapters, we've been tuning the various features of Elgg as per our requirements for socializing. Along with that, customizing the look and feel of our network is also important. In this regard as well, Elgg offers several options.

In this chapter, we'll see how simply by moving around components, individual Elgg users can customize their landing page. We'll also understand Elgg's theming system and create our own themes using Cascading Style Sheets (CSS).

Why Customize?

Elgg ships with a professional looking and slick grayish-blue default theme. Depending on how you want to use Elgg, you'd like your network to have a personalized look. If you are using the network for your own personal use, you really don't care a lot about how it looks.

But if you are using the network as part of your existing online infrastructure, would you really want it to look like every other default Elgg installation on the planet? Of course not! Visitors to your network should easily identify your network and relate it to you.

But theming isn't just about glitter. If you thought themes were all about gloss, think again. A theme helps you "brand" your network. As the underlying technology is the same, a theme is what really separates your network from the others out there.

What Makes Up a Theme?

There are several components that define your network. Let's take a look at the main components and some practices to follow while using them.

- **Colors**: Colors are an important part of your website's identity. If you have an existing website, you'd want your Elgg network to have the same family of colors as your main website. If the two (your website and social network) are very different, the changeover from one to another could be jarring. While this isn't necessary, maintaining color consistency is a good practice.

- **Graphics**: Graphics help you brand the network to make it your own. Every institution has a logo. Using a logo in your Elgg theme is probably the most basic change you'd want to make. But make sure the logo blends in with the theme, that is, it has the same background color.
- **Code**: It takes a little bit of HTML, a sprinkle of PHP, and some CSS magic to manipulate and control a theme.

Controlling Themes

Rather than being single humongous files, themes in Elgg are a bunch of small manageable files. The CSS decoration is separated from the placement code. Before getting our hands dirty creating a theme, let's take a look at the files that control the look and feel of your network. All themes must have these files:

- **A CSS file**: As the name suggests, this file contains all the CSS decorations. You can choose to alter colors and fonts and other elements in this file.
- **A Pageshell file**: In this pageshell file, you define the structure of your Elgg network. If you want to change the position of the Search bar or instead of the standard two-column format, move to a three-column display, this is the file you need to modify.
- **Front page files**: Two files control how the landing page of your Elgg network appears to logged out or logged in users.

- **Optional images folder**: This folder houses all the logos and other artwork that'll be directly used by the theme. Please note that this folder does not include any other graphic elements we've covered in previous chapters such as your picture, or icons to communities, and so on.

The Default Template

Elgg ships with a default template that you can find under your Elgg installation. This is the structure of the files and folders that make up the default template.

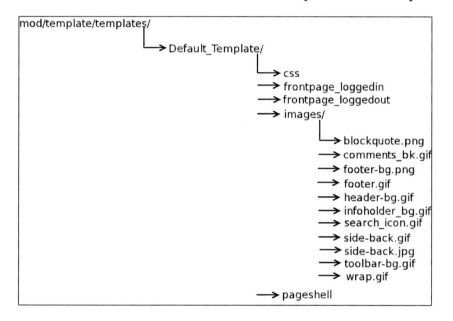

Before we look at the individual files and examine their contents in detail, let's first understand their content in general. All three files, pageshell, frontpage_logedin, and frontpage_loggedout are made up of two types of components.

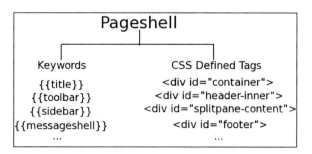

Keywords are used to pull content from the database and display them on the page. Arranging these keywords are the <div> and <span> tags along with several others like <h1>, <ul>, and so on that have been defined in the CSS file.

What are <div> and <span>?

The <div> and <span> are two very important tags especially when it comes to handling CSS files. In a snap, these two tags are used to style arbitrary sections of HTML.

<div> does much the same thing as a paragraph tag <p>, but it divides the page up into larger sections. With <div>, you can also define the style of whole sections of HTML. This is especially useful when you want to give particular sections a different style from the surrounding text.

The <span> tag is similar to the <div> tag. It is also used to change the style of the text it encloses. The difference between <span> and <div> is that a span element is in-line and usually used for a small chunk of in-line HTML.

Both <div> and <span> work with two important attributes, class and id. The most common use of these containers together with the class or id attributes is when this is done with CSS to apply layout, color, and other presentation attributes to the page's content.

In forthcoming sections, we'll see how the two container items use their two attributes to influence themes.

The pageshell

Now, let's dive into understanding the themes. Here's an exact replica of the pageshell of the Default template.

```
<!DOCTYPE html PUBLIC "-//W3C//DTD XHTML 1.0 Transitional//EN"
"http://www.w3.org/TR/xhtml1/DTD/xhtml1-transitional.dtd">
<html xmlns="http://www.w3.org/1999/xhtml">
<head>
<title>{{title}}</title>
        {{metatags}}
</head>
<body>
{{toolbar}}
<div id="container"><!-- open container which wraps the header,
maincontent and sidebar -->
```

```
<div id="header"><!-- open div header -->
   <div id="header-inner">
      <div id="logo"><!-- open div logo -->
      <h1><a href="{{url}}">{{sitename}}</a></h1>
      <h2>{{tagline}}</h2>
      </div><!-- close div logo -->
      {{searchbox}}
   </div>
</div><!-- close div header -->
<div id="content-holder"><!-- open content-holder div -->
   <div id="content-holder-inner">
      <div id="splitpane-sidebar"><!-- open splitpane-sidebar div
-->
         <ul><!-- open sidebar lists -->
         {{sidebar}}
         </ul><!-- close sidebar lists -->
      </div><!-- close splitpane-sidebar div -->
      <div id="splitpane-content"><!-- open splitpane-content div
-->
         {{messageshell}}
         {{mainbody}}
      </div><!-- close open splitpane-content div -->
   </div>
</div><!-- close content-holder div -->
<div id="footer"><!-- start footer -->
   <div id="footer-inner">
      <span style="color:#FF934B">{{sitename}}</span> <a
   href="{{url}}content/terms.php">Terms and
   conditions</a> | <a
   href="{{url}}content/privacy.php">Privacy Policy</a><br />
      <a href="http://elgg.org/"><img src="{{url}}mod/template/
icons/elgg_powered.png" title="Elgg powered" border="0" alt="Elgg
powered" /></a>
      <br />
       {{perf}}
   </div>
</div><!-- end footer -->
</div><!-- close container div -->
</body>
</html>
```

CSS Elements in the pageshell

Phew! That's a lot of mumbo-jumbo. But wait a second! Don't jump to a conclusion! Browse through this section, where we disassemble the file into easy-to-understand chunks. First, we'll go over the elements that control the layout of the pageshell.

`<div id="container">`: This container wraps the complete page and all its elements, including the header, main content, and sidebar. In the CSS file, this is defined as:

```
div#container {
width:940px;
margin:0 auto;
padding:0;
background:#fff;
border-top:1px solid #fff;
}
```

`<div id="header">`: This houses all the header content including the logo and search box.

The CSS definition for the header element:

```
div#header {
margin:0;
padding:0;
text-align:left;
background:url({{url}}mod/template/templates/Default_Template/images/
header-bg.gif) repeat-x;
position:relative;
width:100%;
height:120px;
}
```

The CSS definition for the logo:

```
div#header #logo{
margin: 0px;
padding:10px;
float:left;
}
```

The search box is controlled by the search-header element:

```
div#header #search-header {
float:right;
background:url({{url}}mod/template/templates/Default_Template/images/
search_icon.gif) no-repeat left top;
width:330px;
margin:0;
padding:0;
position:absolute;
top:10px;
right:0;
}
```

`<div id="header-inner">`: While the CSS file of the default template doesn't define the header-inner element, you can use it to control the area allowed to the elements in the header. When this element isn't defined, the logo and search box take up the full area of the header. But if you want padding in the header around all the elements it houses, specify that using this element.

`<div id="content-holder">`: This wraps the main content area.

```
#content-holder {
padding:0px;
margin:0px;
width:100%;
min-height:500px;
overflow:hidden;
position:relative;
}
```

`<div id="splitpane-sidebar">`: In the default theme, the main content area has a two-column layout, split between the content and the sidebar area.

```
div#splitpane-sidebar {
width: 220px;
margin:0;
padding:0;
background:#fff url({{url}}mod/template/templates/Default_Template/
images/side-back.gif) repeat-y;
margin:0;
float: right;
}
div#splitpane-content {
margin: 0;
padding: 0 0 0 10px;
```

```
width:690px;
text-align: left;
color:#000;
overflow:hidden;
min-height:500px;
}
```

`<div id="single-page">`: While not used in the Default template, the content area can also have a simple single page layout, without the sidebar.

```
div#single-page {
margin: 0;
padding: 0 15px 0 0;
width:900px;
text-align: left;
border:1px solid #eee;
}
```

`<div id="content-holder-inner">`: Just like `header-inner`, is used only if you would like a full page layout but a defined width for the actual content.

`<div id="footer">`: Wraps the footer of the page including the links to the terms and conditions and the privacy policy, along with the **Elgg powered** icon.

```
div#footer {
clear: both;
position: relative;
background:url({{url}}mod/template/templates/Default_Template/images/
footer.gif) repeat-x top;
text-align: center;
padding:10px 0 0 0;
font-size:1em;
height:80px;
margin:0;
color:#fff;
width:100%;
}
```

`<div id="footer-inner">`: Like the other `inner` elements, this is only used if you would like a full page layout but restrict the width for the actual footer content.

Other Elements

Apart from the elements used in the pageshell of the default template, there are several others that are defined in the CSS file. Here are some of the most important ones.

For system messages:

```
div#system-message{
border:1px solid #D3322A;
background:#F7DAD8;
color:#000;
padding:3px 50px;
margin:20px 20px 0 20px;
}
```

For the blogging engine:

```
.weblog-post {
margin:20px 0 10px 0;
}
.user {
float:left;
margin:5px 10px 10px 0;
width:105px;
}
.user img {
border:1px solid #eee;
padding:2px;
}
.weblog-keywords p a {
margin:20px 0 0 0;
padding:0;
clear:both;
}
.weblog-title {
margin:10px 0 10px 115px;
}
.post {
margin:10px 0 10px 115px;
background:url({{url}}mod/template/templates/Default_Template/images/
infoholder_bg.gif) left repeat-y;
}
.info {
border:1px solid #ccc;
margin:10px 0 10px 115px;
clear:both;
}
.comment-owner {
border:1px solid #eee;
background:#f2f7fb;
```

```
padding:5px;
margin:20px 0 5px 0;
height:50px;
width:550px;
}
.comment-owner img {
margin:0px 5px 0px 0px;
text-align:left;
}
```

But that's not all. The CSS file is huge. In addition to these elements, the CSS file also defines several other custom tags including custom `<p>`, `<h1>`, `<h2>`, `<ol>`, `<ul>`, `<td>`, etc. But we won't list them here, because they are trivial.

The frontpage Files

In case you got lost in all the CSS code above, let's recap what we've done. We browsed through the pageshell file and learned about the various CSS tags controlling it.

In the next two sections, we'll list the relatively short frontpage files. After that, we'll take on the task to figure out what in the world do the random words in curly braces mean.

The frontpage_loggedout File

```
<h1>Welcome {{name}}</h1>
<p>
This is {{sitename}}, a learning landscape. Why not check out <a
href="{{url}}_weblog/everyone.php">what people are saying</a> right
now?
</p>
<p>
<a href="{{url}}search/tags.php">Find others</a> with similar
interests and
goals.
</p>
<p>
Here are some example users: {{randomusers}}
</p>
<p>
If you like what you see, why not <a href="{{url}}_invite/register.
php">register for an account</a>?
</p>
```

The frontpage_loggedin File

```
<h1>Welcome {{name}}</h1>
<p>
This is {{sitename}}, a learning landscape. Why not check out <a
href="{{url}}_weblog/everyone.php">what people are saying</a> right
now?
</p>
<p>
<a href="{{url}}search/tags.php">Find others</a> with similar
interests and
goals.
</p>
<p>
Here are some example users: {{randomusers}}
</p>
<p>
<a href="{{url}}{{username}}">View your profile</a>! Your portfolio is
the main way people find out about you. You can edit your details and
choose exactly what you want to share with whom.
</p>
```

Content Keywords

Alright, we're here now. In addition to the pageshell, we've listed the two frontpage files. As you see, the `pageshell`, `frontpage_loggedout`, and `frontpage_loggedin` files have lots of keywords. Now, let's look at the various keywords used in them, and understand what kind of information they add to the page:

- `{{title}}`: The title of the network is the same as the name of the site—shows up in the title bar of the browser.
- `{{metatags}}`: Gets the metatags information.
- `{{toolbar}}`: Displays the user navigation toolbar.
- `{{url}}`: The URL of the network.
- `{{sitename}}`: The name of the network as defined while setting up Elgg.
- `{{tagline}}`: The punch line that describes our network. Generally, this appears below the sitename. Again, this too, was defined while setting up Elgg.
- `{{searchbox}}`: This displays the search box with the **Go** button and the **Browse** and **Tag cloud** links.
- `{{sidebar}}`: The sidebar with the user's brief profile and links to his recent activity, friends, and so on.

- {{messageshell}}: This is the area where the system messages appear.
- {{mainbody}}: The main body of the page, where all sorts of information is displayed, depending upon what you are viewing, blog, community, and so on.
- {{name}}: The user's name. If not signed in, this is set to Guest.
- {{randomusers}}: A list of random users who have filled in their profiles, if they exist.

Other Keywords that Can be Used

Just like with the CSS file, there are several other keywords available in addition to the ones listed above. These can be used in either the pageshell or the frontpage files to give more information to logged in or logged out users.

- {{populartags}}: Will list the most popular tags. Same display as in the Tag cloud.
- {{sitemembericons}}: Requires the random site members plug-in, which we'll cover in the next chapter. By default, displays 9 random members. You can also specify a number using {{sitemembericons:x}} where x is the number of users you want to display.
- {{blogsummary:5}}: Displays the latest 5 blog posts within summary format (title, date of posting, and writer's name) with a link to read the detailed entry. Only posts that have been marked as viewable by members of the public are displayed.
- {{blog:5:username}}: This displays the latest 5 posts from a particular user. If you don't include a user {{blog:5}}, this will pull out the 5 latest posts from the network. Posts are displayed in full with the poster's photograph. Again, only posts made available to the public are displayed.

These are some of the basic keywords that are bundled with a regular Elgg installation. Some plug-ins also add their own keywords. We'll mention them along with the respective plug-in.

Hints for Designing a Custom Template

So we've seen all the nuts and bolts that together constitute a theme. They are pretty easy to use. But still, let me show you what you can do with them.

In the following sections, I'll show you how modifying a CSS element or changing the position of a pageshell keyword, will radically change the appearance of your Elgg network.

Pageshell Hacks

A pageshell controls the position and layout of the theme. We can do plenty with it.

Add/Remove Elements

Just as we can move around elements and change their position, you can drop them as well. Also, remember that there are several elements which haven't yet been used in the pageshell or the frontpage files.

For example, let's remove the tagline and instead of the heading, let's display the name of the user. This is useful for designing themes for the community.

Pageshell with Tagline and Site Name

```
<div id="header-inner">
<div id="logo"><!-- open div logo -->
<h1><a href="{{url}}">{{sitename}}</a></h1>
<h2>{{tagline}}</h2>
</div><!-- close div logo -->
{{searchbox}}
</div>
Pageshell without tagline and username as site name
<div id="header-inner">
<div id="logo"><!-- open div logo -->
<h1><a href="{{url}}{{username}}">{{name}}</a></h1>
</div><!-- close div logo -->
{{searchbox}}
</div>
```

In the first code section, the name of the site points to the location of the website. When we replace the sitename with the name of the user, that text should now point to the user's or the community's homepage instead of the homepage of the network. That's why we use the {{url}}{username}} combination. This combination will produce a link to point to the user's landing page.

Add a Copyright Notice

Our footer already has links to our **Terms and Conditions** and **Privacy Policy**. But if you want you can also add some custom text in the footer as well. Several sites use that area to acknowledge the template on which their theme is based. Some use it to add a copyright notice.

Original Footer

```
<div id="footer-inner">
<span style="color:#FF934B">{{sitename}}</span> <a
href="{{url}}content/terms.php">Terms and conditions</
a> | <a href="{{url}}content/privacy.php">Privacy Policy</
a><br />
<a href="http://elgg.org/"><img src="{{url}}mod/template/icons/elgg_
powered.png" title="Elgg powered" border="0" alt="Elgg powered" /></a>
<br />
{{perf}}
</div>
```

Footer with Custom Text

```
<div id="footer-inner"><!-- start footer -->
<span style="color:#FF934B">{{sitename}}</span> <a
href="{{url}}content/terms.php">Terms and conditions</
a> | <a href="{{url}}content/privacy.php">Privacy Policy</
a></p>
<p>&copy; Copyright 2007 - {{sitename}}, All Rights Reserved</p>
<p><a href="http://elgg.org/"><img src="{{url}}mod/template/icons/
elgg_powered.png" title="Elgg powered" border="0" alt="Elgg powered"
/></a></p>
<br />
{{perf}}
</div>
```

CSS Hacks

While pageshell and the frontpage files allow you several customizations, you can only do basic things like shuffling, adding, and removing items. If you want dramatic changes, you'll have to dive into the CSS file. It wouldn't be wrong to say that a theme is actually defined in the CSS file.

Let's explore some quick CSS hacks.

Change Position of Elements

To illustrate changing the position of elements in a theme, let's move over the right-side column to the other side of the page. In order to move the right-side column to the left side, you'll have to change two elements in the CSS file—`splitpane-content` and `splitpane-sidebar`.

Menu Column in the Right-Side

```
div#splitpane-content {
margin: 0;
padding: 0 0 0 10px;
width:690px;
text-align: left;
color:#000;
overflow:hidden;
min-height:500px;
}
div#splitpane-sidebar {
width: 220px;
margin:0;
padding:0;
background:#fff url({{url}}mod/template/templates/Default_Template/
images/side-back.gif) repeat-y;
float: right;
}
```

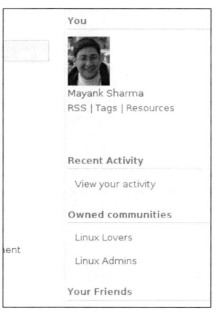

Menu Column in the Left-Side

```
div#splitpane-content {
margin: 10px;
padding 0 0 0 0px;
float:left;
width:560px;
color:#000;
overflow:hidden;
text-align:left;
min-height:500px
}
div#splitpane-sidebar {
float:left;
background:#fff url({{url}}mod/template/templates/Default_Template/
images/side-back.gif) repeat-y;
padding:4px;
margin:0;
width:212px;
}
```

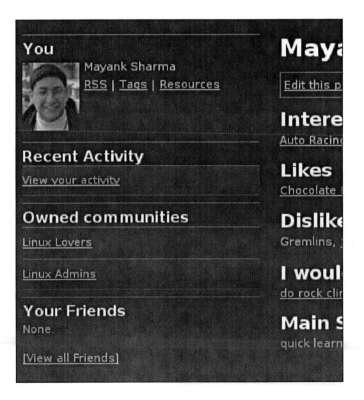

We've changed a couple of things here, but most importantly we've switched the float directions as well as the text alignment.

Fun with Images

The default Elgg theme uses a single color in the body as well as the title background. With a little tweak, you can use an image in the background. Wherever you want to replace the colors with an image, use the background-image option in the CSS.

The Old Logo Definition with Color

```
#logo {
width:220px;
height:100px;
margin:0 10px 0 0;
color:#ccfb86;
float:left;
}
```

The New Logo Definition with an Image called rain.gif

```
#logo {
width:220px;
height:100px;
margin:0 10px 0 0;
background-image:url({{url}}mod/template/templates/Custom_theme/
images/rain.gif);
float:left;
}
```

You can also use a pattern in the background. For that, you don't need to make a huge image. Just make a small image (say 30 pixels by 120 pixels). Now, you can use the repeat-x option.

The New Header Background Definition

```
#header {
width:100%;
height:122px;
background:url({{url}}mod/template/templates/Custom_theme/images/
n1.gif) repeat-x;
}
```

The `repeat-x` option duplicates vertical images, on the X-axis, moving from left to right. If you want to repeat horizontal images (for side-columns) from top to bottom, use the `repeat-y` option.

To add a logo, next to the title of the site, make sure the logo is:

- the size of the site name
- the same color as the background of the header

When you've made a logo that matches this specification, you can use it with the `background-image` option without the `repeat-x` option.

```
#header h1 {
color: White;
letter-spacing: 3px;
font-size: 2.4em;
font-weight: normal;
margin: 10px 0 0 0px;
background: url({{url}}mod/template/templates/Custom_theme/images/
logo.jpg) no-repeat;
padding:0 0 0 30px;
}
```

I have used it with the `<h1>` tag because I'll use my logo next to my site name, which I define with the `<h1>` tag.

Make Body Use More Space

This is a very simple trick. The main content area, including the body and the sidebar are housed within the container `<div>` tag. The default Elgg theme uses a limited space of the container to display the body. You can increase this space by inputting a higher value.

Existing Container Division

```
div#container {
width:940px;
margin:0 auto;
padding:0;
background:#fff;
border-top:1px solid #fff;
}
New container division
div#container {
```

```
width:980px;
margin:0 auto;
padding:0;
background:#fff;
border-top:1px solid #fff;
}
```

You can also specify width in percentage instead of pixels. So, if you want the container to occupy the page fully, specify the width as `width:100%;`.

Hacking Other Themes

There are dozens and dozens of CSS elements we can modify. The best way to understand them is to modify them by hand and see what effect the modifications have on the template.

I'd suggest you to create a folder called `Custom template` under `mod/template/templates/` directory. Then copy the contents of the `Default template` folder into the `Custom template`. Once you have all the files there, open the CSS file and start modifying.

One thing about CSS elements, is that they are interconnected with each other. One element can have a profound effect on its neighboring elements. Therefore, sometimes to achieve a particular customization, you have to modify several elements.

To find out about these connections, try changing the colors and images of the template. Remember to make sure all the colors belong to the same family of colors; else the final result will look like a first grader's art book.

Another trick when playing with colors is to use gradients instead of plain colors. When using gradients, remember to blend the color towards the background color of the template.

Adding Public Templates

Adding templates to your Elgg installation is very simple. Navigate to Elgg's theme repository (`http://elgg.org/themes/files/`). Themes are available as compressed ZIP files:

1. Uncompress the ZIP file. You'll get a folder which contains the pageshell, the CSS files, and all the images used in the theme.

2. Upload this folder to the `mod/template/templates/` directory under your Elgg installation.

3. After the folder has been copied, navigate to the **Change theme** section (under **Account settings**). You'll notice the new theme listed along with the default theme.

Changing Templates

Now that you have a new template in the folder, you can easily use it instead of the Default template.

1. Navigate to the **Change theme** section (under **Account settings**).

2. You'll notice all the themes listed under the **Public Themes** section. Click on the **Preview** button opposite a theme to preview it.

3. When you've previewed a theme, to switch over to it, click on the radio button next to it, scroll down, and click the **Select new theme** button.

Different Themes for Different Areas

The theming system in Elgg is very flexible. Instead of applying a template all over your network, you can choose to use multiple templates to decorate individual parts of Elgg. So, you can use one template for your blog, another one for one of your communities, and another one for some other community.

Select / Create / Edit Themes

Public Themes
The following are public themes that you can use to change the way your My Elgg site looks - these do not change the content only the appearance. Check the preview and then select the one you want. If you wish you can adapt one of these using the 'create theme' option below.

○	**Custom template**	Preview
○	**Default Template**	Preview
○	**Differential**	Preview
○	**Mandarin**	Preview
○	**Nonzero-blue**	Preview
⦿	**TrulySimple**	Preview
○	orage juice	Preview

Change templates

The selected changes will affect:

☑	**User page**	**Your personal space**
☐	**Linux Lovers**	**Community: Linux Lovers**
☑	**Linux Admins**	**Community: Linux Admins**

Select new theme

To do this, follow the instructions in the previous section and upload templates to your Elgg installation:

1. Navigate to the **Change the** section (under **Account settings**).

2. You'll notice all the themes listed under the **Public Themes** section. Click on the **Preview** button opposite a theme to preview it.

3. When you've previewed a theme, to switch over to it, click on the radio button next to it.

4. Now scroll down to the **Change templates** section. Under this section, Elgg will list all the areas of Elgg you have control over. Select the section or sections you want to apply this template to, by clicking the checkbox next to them.

5. Finally, click the **Select new theme** button to apply the template.

6. Repeat the process to apply another template to another section of your network.

Creating Themes Based on Templates

What we've been creating up until now were templates. These are broad specifications on which themes are based. In a template, we define all the possible elements in the CSS and pageshell. As in the case of the default template, many of the CSS elements were never used. Based on these broad templates, users can design their own custom themes, which they can apply in their blogs, or communities.

Creating Themes

To create a theme, log in to your account and go into the **Account settings** section, by clicking on that link in the top navigation bar. From inside here:

1. Click the **Change theme** link.

2. Scroll down to the **Create theme** section, and enter a theme name in the space provided.

3. From the pull down menu, under the **Based on** section, select the template you want to base your theme on.

4. Click the **Create Theme** button and Elgg will copy over the template into your custom theme.

Create theme

Here you can create your own themes based on one of the existing public themes. Just select which public theme you would like to alter and then create your own. You will now have edit privilages.

Theme name

| Yellow Brick Road |

Based on

| orage juice ▾ |

Create Theme

Once you have created a custom template, follow the suggestions from the **Hints for designing a custom template** section and tweak the template.

Validating Themes

According to the World Wide Web Consortium (W3C) (`http://www.w3c.org/`), validation is a process of checking your documents against a formal Standard, such as those published by W3C for HTML and XML-derived Web document types, or by the WapForum for WML, and so on.

It's important for themes to be validated, because you want any browser to understand and display them properly. As per W3C, non-validated themes will not only display improperly, but can also confuse the browser enough to cause it to crash.

W3C has a couple of free online validating services for checking your HTML (`http://validator.w3.org/`) and CSS (`http://jigsaw.w3.org/css-validator/`) code. The service can check pages that are already online or HTML and CSS files residing on your computer. If you have trouble using the validators, refer to their manual (`http://validator.w3.org/docs/help.html#manual`).

Replacing the Default Template

Once you have a custom theme, it's only natural that you'd want all your visitors and members to see that, rather than Elgg's Default template.

To replace Elgg's default template, you'll have to move your custom theme inside the `mod/template/templates/Default_Theme/` folder. This is because Elgg is programmed to use whatever theme's under the `Default_Theme` folder as the network default.

Initially, prepare your custom theme under a folder of its own. Once it's completed, simply overwrite the contents of the `Default_Theme` folder with your new CSS, `pageshell`, `frontpage_loggedout`, `frontpage_loggedin`, and `images` folder.

Contributing Themes

As a free and open source project, Elgg is powered by your contributions. The area that receives most public contributions for web-based projects is themes. You too can contribute your custom themes to Elgg's repository for others to customize and use.

According to the Elgg documentation, before submitting a theme, make sure you follow these guidelines, for the theme to be accepted:

1. Must be validated using the WC3 CSS Validator (`http://jigsaw.w3.org/css-validator/`).

2. Every effort should be made to make the theme cross-browser compatible. If the theme is designed for a particular browser or doesn't render well on another, please clearly label and or mention this while submitting the theme.

3. The theme should be housed in a folder named after the theme. This folder should contain a CSS file and pageshell plus an images folder (if applicable). Do not hardcode links to images in the CSS file. Use the `{{URL}}` keyword to point to images used in your theme. For example: `{{URL}}mod/template/templates/Custom_theme/images/searchbox.gif`

Summary

In this chapter, we've looked at Elgg's theming engine. We've understood and studied its nuts and bolts by examining in detail the four files that give it structure and influence its design—the pageshell, the CSS file, and the two frontpage files.

I've also shared some tips and tricks you can use to start playing around with the existing themes. We've also discussed a few general tips one needs to keep in mind while designing a theme. A theme isn't a random splash of colors! You need to spend decent time designing your theme, because it creates recall, gives it an identity, and associates your network with you.

To complement the default theme, you can also get themes from Elgg's website. You can also use these themes to base your custom theme on from inside Elgg. If one theme isn't enough for your network, you can give users the freedom to apply whichever theme they please to different areas of the network.

7
Elgg Plug-Ins

Throughout the book, I've raved about Elgg's features. Despite having malleable features that you can use to tweak Elgg as per your requirements, it might fall short on certain points. But thanks to the clever developers of Elgg, it has been designed to take on new features. Think of a basic Elgg install as a core that has enough features to get you started. Depending on your particular requirements, you can add layers and layers of plug-ins over this core.

Just like themes and templates, plug-ins allow you to personalize your network. But this type of personalization is different. While templates and themes decorate the exterior, plug-ins personalize it by extending the core functionality of the network.

Elgg has an active plug-in community that churns out plug-ins by the dozen. There are several types of plug-ins. Some plug-ins that are important to almost any social network have been covered in previous chapters. For example, blog spam prevention plug-ins have been covered in Chapter 4. Wiki and Message plug-ins have been covered in Chapter 5. These plug-ins add functionality that help make your Elgg installation a better, cleaner, and more collaborative social network.

In this chapter, we will cover some plug-ins whose requirement varies from network to network. You may or may not want to implement these plug-ins. Don't get me wrong. They all do provide excellent features and are very powerful. But depending on your network, your users might find them very useful or just a distraction.

General Structures of Plug-Ins

All plug-ins under Elgg follow guidelines laid out by the developers of Elgg. The plug-ins are available in a compressed format. Some are available as tarballs (with `.tar.gz` extension) and some as ZIP files (with `.zip` extension). To use the plug-ins, you'll need to uncompress them.

Under Windows, the freely available WinZip program will be able to uncompress both `.tar.gz` files as well as `.zip` files. In Linux, the tar and unzip utilities will uncompress both the tarball and the ZIP file respectively.

After uncompressing, the plug-ins need to be placed under their respective directories under the mod/ (for modules) directory of the Elgg installation. So let's assume that on your web server, Elgg is installed under `/var/www/elgg/`. In this case, the plug-in will be under `/var/www/elgg/mod/<plugin-1>`.

Depending on the plug-in, the plug-in directory will contain several files and sub-directories. But all of them will contain a `lib.php` file. This is the file that defines the core functionality of the plug-in. In addition to this file, there will be some documentation, either a README file, or an INSTALL file, or a `plugin.info` file that describes the plugin and carries instructions for installing or upgrading the plug-in.

Things to Remember While Installing Plug-Ins

Installing plug-ins is a walk in the park. But, there are certain things that (as we'll see later on in the chapter), you could get your hands burnt with if you aren't careful. Here are a few guidelines:

1. Try on a non-live installation first. Before you deploy a plug-in on the main "production" network, it's a good idea to test the plug-in by installing it on an offline, local installation of Elgg. This will test and tweak the plug-in and save the trouble of uninstalling, if it doesn't work for you.

2. Never delete. Several plug-ins will ask you to manually change certain lines of text in various configurations and code files. When replacing text in any of the critical files, never delete the existing lines. Only comment them out, with a note saying the lines have been commented out because of the XYZ plug-in. Again, this helps you if the plug-in malfunctions and you need to revert the network back to its original state.

3. Comment on any new additions. Similarly, when appending new lines of code in various files, make it a point to add detailed comments on the plug-in that has asked for these lines of code to be appended.

4. Maintain a list of steps taken to install a plug-in. This is the most crucial of all steps. While the plug-in has installation instructions, and I've also detailed them in the following sections in this chapter, it's a good idea to note each and every step you take while installing a plug-in. Note what files you've modified, what sections were removed or commented out, the name of the plug-in's directory, and so on. This will come in handy when removing or upgrading plug-ins.

The Plug-Ins

Now that we have a fair idea of how plug-ins operate in Elgg, let's cut to the chase and browse some plug-ins. There are all sorts of plug-ins in the section below. The plug-ins we begin with will help you administrate your network better. Then, we cover some plug-ins that help you modify your blog and make it more reader-friendly. We also take a look at some plug-ins that equip us with keywords, which we can use in any of the three template files (pageshell and the two frontpage files).

Maintenance Mode

The maintenance mode plug-in comes into play when you have to take the network offline for maintenance work. Common maintenance tasks include backing up the site database, and upgrading from one Elgg version to a newer version. You wouldn't want users to log into the network and create content, while you are busy backing up data.

The maintenance plug-in is a simple plug-in which, when activated, only allows the administrator to log in. All other users aren't allowed to log into the system. The plug-in also displays a message warning the users that the network is under maintenance and that only system administrators are allowed inside.

> The system is in maintenance mode, only can login system administrators. Would be back to normal operation soon.
>
> **Log On**
> _____
> Please log in

To use the plug-in, download it `http://elgg.org/mod/plug-ins/plugin.php?id=39` and unzip it under Elgg's `mod/` directory.

Then log in as the administrator and click the **Administration** link. In the links on this page, you'll notice an additional **Activate Maintenance Mode** link. Before starting the maintenance work, click on this link to stop/disallow users from logging in. To restore operations, log in as the administrator, head over to the **Administration** section and click the **Deactivate Maintenance Mode** link to open the site to users.

Custom Metatags in Header

As we know by now, one of Elgg's strong points is that it allows users to easily design and change their templates and themes. But this ability of Elgg can be a disadvantage when you, the administrator, want to maintain consistency in the invisible section of the template — the header.

But with the Custom Metatags plug-in, you can specify custom pieces of code that the plug-in will include in all page headers, irrespective of the template the users might be running. Just grab the plug-in [http://elgg.org/mod/plugins/plugin. php?id=16], uncompress it, and copy its contents under Elgg's mod/ directory. Under the uncompressed plug-in directory, you'll notice an empty file called metatags. inc. The contents of this file are replicated in headers across templates. So just paste your code in this file and you're done.

To illustrate, let me use an old piece of JavaScript code to resize the window as per my dimensions. This is a technique that I used in my early web development years. It involves specifying the dimensions of the window using a JavaScript function. Importantly though, this piece of code needs to be placed in the header of the page (between the <head> and </head> tags).

For controlling our Elgg windows, we'll use the metatags.inc file provided by the Custom Metatags plug-in and copy-paste this code in it:

```
<!-- The first number is the width; the second is the height. -->
<script>
self.resizeTo(1024,768);
</script>
```

Now open your browser and log in to your Elgg network. As soon as the page starts to load, the browser will run the JavaScript and resize itself to 1024x768. This will happen irrespective of the section of the network you're viewing or the template you are using. Also, if you view the source of the page (*Ctrl+U* in Firefox), you'll notice the script (and the comment) on every page on the network.

EasyJoin

The default Elgg registration is a two-step process. To recall, users first visit the network and enter their real name and email address. Then, Elgg on behalf of your network, sends them an invitation email with a link to enter other information like a username and password, before allowing them to log in.

The EasyJoin plug-in helps you simplify the registration process. It takes the email invitation aspect out of the equation. Members interested in joining your network will be able to instantaneously register into your network if you use this plug-in.

◆ My Elgg site terms and conditions
◆ Privacy policy

Your name

Your username - (Must be letters only)

Your email address

Enter a password

Your password again for verification purposes

☐ I am at least thirteen years of age.

Join

Download the plug-in [http://elgg.org/mod/plug-ins/plugin.php?id=38] and unzip it under Elgg's mod/ directory. But to use this plug-in, you need to change the link of the registration page in your network.

You'll need to modify three files and make these changes:

1. Edit units/display/function_log_on_pane.php. Change link in $reg_link to mod/easyjoin/register.php.

2. Edit lib/displaylib.php. Change link in $reg_link to mod/easyjoin/register.php.

3. Edit frontpage_loggedout file in your template and change the registration link from {{url}}_invite/register.php to {{url}}mod/easyjoin/register.php.

Now, when unregistered users land up on the main page and click on the link to register, they'll be shown a different registration page than Elgg's default registration page. Using this new page, the users will be able to enter their registration information and use it to log in as soon as they are done registering.

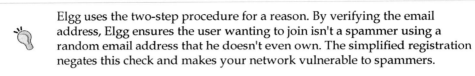

Elgg uses the two-step procedure for a reason. By verifying the email address, Elgg ensures the user wanting to join isn't a spammer using a random email address that he doesn't even own. The simplified registration negates this check and makes your network vulnerable to spammers.

Related Posts

Most blogs carry links to other posts on the blog. The Related Posts plug-in eases navigation between blog posts. The plug-in adds links to help readers move to the next and previous posts in that blog. Additionally, it also adds links to posts related to the one that's being read. These related posts can be from this blog or from other blogs across the network.

```
Some related posts:

This weblog                          Others weblogs

   • New Wave of Hard Discs            • No related posts
   • Motorola A780 is a sight to behold
```

To install the plug-in, grab it [http://elgg.org/mod/plug-ins/plugin.php?id=31], unzip and copy contents to Elgg's mod/ directory.

Before you can use the plug-in, you need to modify your Elgg database to make space for storing the related posts information. For this, log in into your network as the administrator and point your browser to this location [http://<your-elgg-network>/mod/relatedposts/dbsetup.php]. You should see messages like these printed on the screen:

(mysql): ALTER TABLE elggweblog_posts ADD FULLTEXT relatedposts (title, body)

Success

(mysql): SELECT name FROM elggdatalists WHERE name = 'relatedposts_ dbsetup'

(mysql): SHOW COLUMNS FROM 'elggdatalists'

(mysql): INSERT INTO elggdatalists (name, value) VALUES ('relatedposts_ dbsetup', 1)

(mysql): SELECT LAST_INSERT_ID()

This means your database has been modified successfully.

Now, you need to modify the code of the page that displays the blog post to make it display the related posts information. In version 0.8, you need to edit the file `mod/blog/lib/weblogs_posts_view.php`. Around line 149, you'll see this piece of code:

```
if (isset($individual) && ($individual == 1)) {
    // looking at an individual post and its comments
        $commentsbody = "";
```

We need to add two lines of code here. Replace this section with the following code:

```
if (isset($individual) && ($individual == 1)) {
    // looking at an individual post and its comments
    // Relatedpost plug-in
    $links .= run('mod:relatedposts:show', $post);
    $commentsbody = "";
```

That's it! Now head back to any blog on your network and open a post. You'll notice the new navigation links just before the comments section.

Tag Suggest and Autocomplete

One aspect of online cataloging systems that rely on users to tag information is that they might end up with similar sounding or abbreviated tags. For example, some people might use the tag "technology", others may use the tag "tech". This dilutes information in several tags, hurting its chances of being accessed.

With the Tag Suggest plug-in, you can avoid this situation. Once the plug-in is in use, it'll suggest tags and autocomplete it for them. So if a user wants to tag a technology piece, as soon as he types the letters "tec..", the plug-in will kick in and display all the related tags that are in use in the system, like "technology". While the user can still ignore the suggestion and tag the information as "tech", this plug-in ensures better cataloging of information.

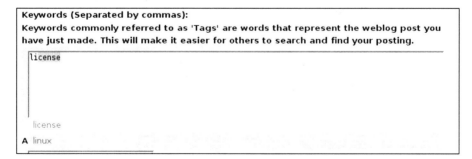

To use the plug-in, just grab it [http://elgg.org/mod/plug-ins/plugin.php?id=33], and unzip it under Elgg's mod/ directory. Now, when you key in tags, you'll be prompted to use one of the existing ones in the system.

Internally, the plug-in searches for tags from various sources. By default, it looks for all public and loggedin weblog tags. The other options available are:

-1: all system tags (includes private tags)

0: all system public/loggedin tags

1: all system public/loggedin weblog tags (default)

2: all user tags (includes tags of user's communities)

4: all user weblog tags (same as **1** but only weblog type)

To make the plug-in use a specific tag group, edit the config.php files under the plug-ins directory (<elgg-install>/mod/tagsuggest/config.php). In future, there will be another option to restrict to all of the blog owner's tags.

Blog Categories

Elgg files data using keywords. Blog posts too, among other things, as we've seen throughout the chapters, are categorized and tagged with keywords. The advantage of tagging keywords with elements is that it makes finding all types of data easier. By searching for a particular keyword, Elgg will find you blog posts, files, presentations, and even users that have that keyword in their profile.

Traditionally, though, blogs have always filed posts under certain categories. Think of categories as broad topics that categorize your blog. Categories are a reader-friendly feature. Readers that come across your blog can get a quick snapshot of the topics you blog about, by looking at the categories.

Blog categories
admin
news
scripts
security
tips

The Weblog Categories plug-in does exactly this. It adds a sidebar to your blog, which lists the topics you like to blog about. By clicking on these topics, the reader will see all the posts filed under this category. To install the plug-in, download it [http://elgg.org/mod/plug-ins/plugin.php?id=2] and extract it under Elgg's mod/ directory.

After installing the plug-in, log in to your network and head to your blog. The plug-in would have added a new link to your blogging toolbar called **Manage blog categories**. Filing your existing blog entries in categories doesn't require much effort. Neither do you have to make any changes or take extra steps while writing new posts. So how are they filed under categories?

Manage blog categories

🔊 | Post a new entry | View blog | Archive | Friends' blogs | Interesting posts | View all posts | Manage blog categories

Categories allow you to highlight particular tags that represent important weblog content and display them in your sidebar.

For example, if you wanted to draw attention to all blog posts tagged with 'science', you could add that tag below, and users would know that 'science' represents an important category of content. They could then click on 'science' in your sidebar and see all content relating to science.

To set up categories, type the tags you'd like to highlight separated by commas below:

Highlighted categories

admin, news, scripts, security, tips

Save

It' actually pretty simple. The categories are nothing but keywords that you've already used to tag posts. In the blog categories section added by the plug-in, you'll notice a huge text box. Just enter the keywords you'd like to be listed in your blog's sidebar and you're done.

Spend a little time deciding your categories. Ideally, categories are much broader in nature than keywords. Cricket, football, physics, are good keywords and sports, science are good categories.

Forwarder

By default, when someone visits a user's page, they land on their profile. While a profile is a great place to let visitors know more about you and make friends, after a while it would make more sense to take them elsewhere. For example, regular visitors or your friends might be interested in visiting your blog rather than being shown the same old profile again and again.

The Forwarder plug-in is designed to do exactly that. Using this plug-in, you can make your visitor land on another page than your profile. Not only that, as a bonus, you can also use the plug-in to define an easy to remember name for your landing page.

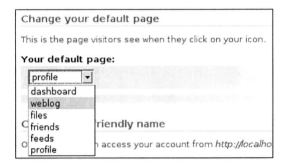

To use the plug-in, download it [`http://elgg.org/mod/plug-ins/plugin.php?id=3`] and extract its content under Elgg's `mod/` directory. Next, you need to make Elgg aware of this new customized landing page plug-in and how to deal with it. Open Elgg's `.htaccess` file, locate the first `RewriteRule` line and before it, append these lines:

```
## RewriteRules for forwarder plug-in
RewriteRule ^([A-Za-z0-9]+)(\/)?$ mod/forwarder/landing.php?profile_
name=$1
RewriteRule ^home\/([A-Za-z0-9]+)(\/)?$ mod/forwarder/friendly.
php?profile_name=$1
RewriteRule ^([A-Za-z0-9]+)\/profile(\/)?$ profile/index.php?profile_
name=$1
## End
```

This installs the plug-in. Now, log into your Elgg account and click the **Account settings** link in the top panel. At the end of the **Edit user details** page, you'll notice two new sections. The **Change your default page** will let you choose the landing page from one of the following:

Dashboard

Weblog

Files

Friends

Feeds

Profile

Change your friendly name

Once set, you can access your account from *http://localhost/elgg/home/[your friendly name]/*

Your friendly name:

bodhi

Make your selection and move to the **Change your friendly name** section. In the field provided, enter the friendly name that affects your URL. For example, use Elgg's original naming scheme, the location to your weblog would be `http://<elgg-url>/<username>/weblog`. If you use a friendly name, and choose to use the blog as your landing page, the URL would be: `http://<elgg-url>/home/<your friendly name>`.

Comment Wall

Blogs are an effective way for communicating with your audience. But there's another easier way. It's called a Comment Wall. As the name suggests, people use the Comment Wall to write comments to you. Unlike a blog, where people comment on what you've written, a Comment Wall is a place to scribble random messages to the owner.

The Comment Wall plug-in adds a widget to your existing repository of widgets that you can use to customize your landing page. Install the plug-in by downloading it [`http://elgg.org/mod/plug-ins/plugin.php?id=22`] and unzipping under Elgg's `mod/` directory.

To use the plug-in, head over to the **Your Profile** section and click the **Add widget** link. When you select and add the comment wall widget, you can customize the wall to display a specific number of comments. The plug-in also allows you to decide who gets to comment on your wall. You can either restrict only logged-in users to comment or be liberal and allow members of the public to write on your wall.

Comment Wall

How many comments would you like to appear?

6

Change the privacy level of your comment wall.

Access: Private ▼ Save widget

You can also use the Comment Wall to post small updates about your network. By marking the Comment Wall as private, only you can scribble on your wall. This gives you a space to mention brief changes or updates you've made to the network or post links to interesting articles or online videos. So basically, you can use it for scribbling anything that doesn't deserve a complete blog post.

Recent Comments Keyword

In Chapter 6, we had covered several keywords. We used them to display all sorts of information in the pageshell and in the `frontpage_loggedout` and `frontpage_loggedin` files.

The Recent Comments Keyword plug-in adds another type of keyword to that list—`recentcomments`. As its name suggests, this keyword will display the recent comments that have been added in the system.

And some recent comments:

- "yeh really!" by kbronx about five minutes ago at Post with a file
- "when do you think this will be available? &nb..." by gad-get about five minutes ago at New Wave of Hard Discs

To install the plug-in, download it [http://elgg.org/mod/plug-ins/plugin. php?id=21] and unzip its contents inside Elgg's mod/ directory. That's all.

You can use the plug-in in three modes:

{{recentcomments}}: Displays 5 recent comments in the system.

{{recentcomments:X}}: Display X number of recent comments.

{{recentcomments:X:N}}: Displays X number of recent comments but trimmed to N number of characters.

Logged In Users

Wouldn't it be nice if your users could find out whether their friends on the network are online as well, when they log in? Social networking websites have different mechanisms for letting their users know which of their peers are also logged into the system.

The Logged in Users plug-in equips you with another very useful keyword. You can use this keyword to print a list of all the users logged into the system.

To install the plug-in, just grab it [http://elgg.org/mod/plug-ins/plugin.php?id=24], uncompress and upload its contents to Elgg's mod/ directory. Now you can use the **{{loggedinusers}}** keyword in the pageshell or in the frontpage files.

There are two possible locations where you can append the keyword. You can use it in the frontpage_loggedin file. As soon as users log in to the network, they'll be taken to the landing page controlled by the frontpage_loggedin file. Having the keyword on this page, will give users an opportunity to instantly find out whether their friends are online too.

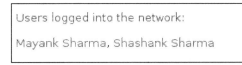

The other location is at the bottom of the pageshell. You can use this keyword in your footer section to display all the logged in users just above the copyright notice. Now that you have the information here, users will have access to the list of logged in users on every section of the network.

Icons of Site Members

If you go to Eduspaces.net (running on and by the same people who develop Elgg) you'll notice that in addition to displaying random users, it also displays their icons. Since people choose wacky icons, wouldn't it be cool if you too could display icons of users on your network?

The Sitemembers plug-in provides a template keyword that you can place in your pageshell or frontpage files. Just grab the plug-in, untar it, and copy its contents to Elgg's `mod/` directory. That's all there is to installation!

Now head over to one of the three templates. I'll demonstrate by adding the following lines to the `frontpage_loggedout` file:

```
Some users from the network:
{{sitemembericons}}
```

If you want to restrict the number of icons displayed by the keyword, you can specify the number with it. For example, `{{sitemembericons:6}}` will display icons of 6 members. But remember, the keyword will only display icons belonging to people. It will not show communities.

Calendar

Depending on how you are using the network, a Calendar can be a great addition to your network. You can use a calendar to add appointments and events. A calendar on a social network, doesn't only remind you of your important tasks, but also your community and friends if it's a group task.

Elgg's Calendar plug-in is quite simple and straightforward to use. You can use it to set personal events as well as community events and events with your friends. Of course, the real benefit of social calendaring, is with the community and friends calendar's in which other people in your network (community and friend list) can also add events. These keep everyone updated of events that involve more people than you — think Sunday race day at your local race track with friends or Friday afternoon lunch at the office with the team.

To install the Calendar, download the plug-in [`http://elgg.org/mod/plug-ins/plugin.php?id=17`] and unzip in within Elgg's `mod/` directory. Now open the htaccess-calendar from inside the unzipped directory and copy its contents into Elgg's `.htaccess` file. These are nothing but a set of rewrite rules.

Next, create a directory called `export` in Elgg's data directory that is kept outside of the Elgg's web server directory and make it writeable.

```
cd <elgg-data-directory>
mkdir export
chmod 777 export
```

Finally, log in to your Elgg network as the administrator. The plug-in will automatically update the respective database tables to make space for the calendar data. Once you get into your network, you'll notice a new **Your Calendar** link in your top navigation bar. The Calendar plug-in adds links to view your personal calendar as well as links to view the community and friends calendar. The plug-in also adds a RSS feed of your calendar that others can subscribe to keep up-to-date with changes in your schedule.

Mayank Sharma :: Calendar

rss | Archives | View Calendar | Add New Event | My Community Events | My Friends Events

	<<		July 2007			>>
Sunday	**Monday**	**Tuesday**	**Wednesday**	**Thursday**	**Friday**	**Saturday**
1	2	3	4	5	6	7
8	9	10	11	12	13	14
15	16	17	18 Revision deadline	19	20	21

Adding an Event

To add an event to the calendar, you can either locate the date in the visual calendar and click the date or use the **Add New Event** link. Whatever method you choose, the plug-in will launch the **Add calendar event** page.

This page has a form with fields to input details regarding the event, like a title, start and stop time, event location, and event description. You'll also have the opportunity to change the date for the event, irrespective of how you got to this page. If you got here by clicking a particular date, the calendar is aware of the date you want to set the event for.

You can manually enter the date in two ways. One option is to select the year, month and date from a pull down menu. The other option is to use the JavaScript pop-up calendar that you see on online ticketing websites.

Add A Calendar Event

Event Title:

Lunch@Work

Date

20 ▾ July ▾ 2007 ▾ ▦

Time

Start 1 ▾ 0 ▾ pm ▾ End 0 ▾ 0 ▾ pm ▾

Event Location:

Hotel Prescott @ Kent Gardens

Event Description:

Meet with team to discuss the new project.

Active Calendar Cle _ ▢ ✕

◈   **July 2007**   ➡

Sun	Mon	Tue	Wed	Thu	Fri	Sat
1	2	3	4	5	6	7
8	9	10	11	12	13	14
15	16	17	18	19	20	21
22	23	24	25	26	27	28
29	30	31				

Close Calendar

Keywords (Separated by commas):
Keywords commonly referred to as 'Tags' are words that represent the calendar post you have just made. This will make it easier for others to search and find your posting.

team, lunch, meeting

Access restrictions:

Private ▾

Save Event

Like any data on the network, you can use keywords to describe the event as well and restrict access to it. Once you've entered all the information, click on the **Save Event** button to add the event to your calendar.

Upcoming Events

Adding events in the calendar is just one part of the puzzle. Being reminded of the events is necessary too. The Calendar plug-in does a good job of logging your events and exporting them into your calendaring applications. It can also turn your calendar into a RSS feed.

But if you want a reminder of your scheduled events, you'll have to use another plug-in. The upcoming events plug-in does exactly what it sounds like—alerts you of upcoming scheduled calendar events. And it does so by making available a keyword that you can use in the frontpage files or pageshell.

Remember to first install the Calendar plug-in before using this plug-in. The plug-in pulls information from the Elgg tables that were modified by the Calendar plug-in to record the calendar's event-related information. Once the calendar plug-in is running, all you have to do, is grab the upcoming events plug-in [`http://elgg.org/mod/plug-ins/plugin.php?id=25`], and extract it under Elgg's `mod/` directory.

Upcoming events:

* Football coaching on July 16, 2007 (Mon) happens in about an hour or two
* Revision deadline on July 19, 2007 (Thu) happens in 3 days
* Lunch@Work on July 20, 2007 (Fri) happens in 4 days
* Pickup Bryan on July 27, 2007 (Fri) happens next week

Now open the pageshell or `frontpage_loggedin` or `frontpage_loggedout` files and use the `{{upcomingevents}}` keyword. It's not a bad idea to notify a user of his upcoming events when he logs into the network. For that just open the `frontpage_loggedin` file and at the bottom on the page enter this line of code:

```
<p>Upcoming events: {{upcomingevents}}</p>
```

This will display all upcoming events. You can also limit the number of events displayed by appending a number to the keyword. For example, `{{upcomingevents:3}}` will restrict the number of events to display to 3.

How to Remove Plug-Ins

We've seen how easy it is to go beyond Elgg's core functionality by using plug-ins. Installing them isn't too difficult either! All that is required for most plug-ins is to download them, unzip, and copy to your Elgg installation. But removing plug-ins can be a mini-challenge, especially if you didn't exercise caution while installing them.

That's because there's no predefined mechanism for removing plug-ins. To remove a plug-in, you have to retrace its installation steps in reverse. But be careful and be thorough. Of course, you can just remove the plugin's directory from under the `mod/` directory. But that'll leave rogue pieces of unused code in your templates and configuration files that may cause problems later.

Upgrading Plug-Ins

As Elgg continues to evolve, so do the plug-ins. New versions of plug-ins keep popping up every now and then with new functionalities, improvements in code, and so on. Before upgrading Elgg itself, ensure your plug-ins work with the new version. Keep an eye on the Elgg plug-in community for changes and upgrades to the plug-ins.

Almost all the plug-ins we've covered in this section and throughout the book have clear and documented upgrading policies. When you download a newer version of the plug-in, you'll notice they contain instructions for upgrading your version of the plug-in to the latest version. These instructions vary from plug-in to plug-in.

For a complex plug-in like the Calendar, that requires changes to the database while installing, all I did to upgrade from 0.1 to 0.7 was replace the contents of the plug-in under the mod/ directory. Similarly, the keyword plug-ins, only require unpacking new contents into their respective mod/ directories. The upgraded plug-in might provide new features in terms of new options. For example, a new version of the sitemembers plug-in might add a new option to display communities in addition to members as it does now. So, in addition to upgrading the plug-in you'll have to make appropriate changes to the implementation of the plug-in as well.

Summary

The great thing about Elgg's design is its ability to take on new features thanks to these small pieces of code. In this chapter, we have covered some interesting plug-ins. Except for the three interaction plug-ins, the other plug-ins in this chapter might or might not be of use to everyone; after all, online foums and sharing thoughts,bookmarks, and emails are some of the very important functions of a network.

We have covered plug-ins that help you display a message when your site is under maintenance and other such plug-ins that'll allow you to better control and administrate your network. We have also covered a few plug-ins designed to help readers of your blog by allowing them to browse through posts. Some plug-ins in this chapter also dealt with providing you with keywords to display more information to logged in or visitors to your network. They provide both information and do their part in inducing new users to join the network.

A
Installing Elgg

In addition to its impressive feature list, Elgg is an admin's dolly. It can install in the popular Linux web application rollout stack of Linux, Apache, MySQL, and PHP, fondly referred to as LAMP. As MySQL and PHP can run under Windows operating system as well, you can set up Elgg to serve your purpose for such an environment.

Setting Up LAMP

Let's look at setting up the Linux, Apache, MySQL, PHP web server environment. There are several reasons for the LAMP stack's popularity. While most people enjoy the freedom offered by these Open Source software, small business and non-profits will also be impressed by its procurement cost: $0.

Step 1: Install Linux

The critical difference between setting up Elgg under Windows or Linux is installing the operating system. The Linux distribution I'm using to set up Elgg is Ubuntu Linux (http://www.ubuntu.com/). It's available as a free download and has a huge and active global community, should you run into any problems.

Covering step-by-step installation of Ubuntu Linux is too much of a digression for this book. Despite the fact that Ubuntu isn't too difficult to install, because of its popularity there are tons of installation and usage documentation available all over the Web. Linux.com has a set of videos that detail the procedure of installing Ubuntu (http://www.linux.com/articles/114152). Ubuntu has a dedicated help section (https://help.ubuntu.com/) for introduction and general usage of the distribution.

Step 2: Install Apache

Apache is the most popular web server used on the Internet. Reams and reams of documents have been written on installing Apache under Linux. Apache's documentation sub-project (`http://httpd.apache.org/docs-project/`) has information on installing various versions of Apache under Linux.

Ubuntu, based on another popular Linux distribution, Debian, uses a very powerful and user-friendly packaging system. It's called apt-get and can install an Apache server within minutes. All you have to do is open a terminal and write this command telling apt-get what to install:

```
apt-get install apache2 apache2-common apache2-doc apache2-mpm-prefork
apache2-utils libapr0 libexpat1 ssl-cert
```

This will download Apache and its most essential libraries. Next, you need to enable some of Apache's most critical modules:

```
a2enmod ssl
```

```
a2enmod rewrite
```

```
a2enmod include
```

The rewrite module is critical to Elgg, so make sure it's enabled, else Elgg wouldn't work properly.

That's it. Now, just restart Apache with: `/etc/init.d/apache2 restart`.

Step 3: MySQL

Installing MySQL isn't too much of an issue either. Again, like Ubuntu and Apache, MySQL can boast of a strong and dedicated community. This means there's no dearth of MySQL installation or usage related documentation (`http://www.mysql.org/doc/`).

If you're using MySQL under Ubuntu, like me, installation is just a matter of giving apt-get a set of packages to install:

```
apt-get install mysql-server mysql-client libmysqlclient12-dev
```

Finally, set up a password for MySQL with:

```
mysqladmin -h yourserver.example.com -u root password
yourrootmysqlpassword
```

Step 4: Install PHP Support

You might think I am exaggerating things a little bit here, but I kid you not, PHP is one of the most popular and easy to learn languages for writing web applications. Why do you think we are setting up out Linux web server environment to execute PHP? It's because Elgg itself is written in PHP! And so are hundreds and thousands of other web applications.

So I'm sure you've guessed by now that PHP has a good deal of documentation (http://www.php.net/docs.php) as well. You've also guessed it's now time to call upon Ubuntu's apt-get package manager to set up PHP:

```
apt-get install libapache2-mod-php5 php5 php5-common php5-gd php5-mysql
php5-mysqli
```

As you can see, in addition to PHP, we are also installing packages that'll hook up PHP with the MySQL database and the Apache web server.

That's all there is to setting up the LAMP architecture to power your Elgg network.

Setting Up WAMP

If you are used to Microsoft's Windows operating system or want to avoid the extra minor learning curve involved with setting up the web server on a Linux distribution, especially, if you haven't done it before, you can easily replicate the Apache, MySQL, PHP web server on a Windows machine. Cost wise, all server components—the Apache web server, MySQL database, and the PHP development language—have freely available Windows versions as well. But the base component of this stack, the operating system, Microsoft Windows, isn't.

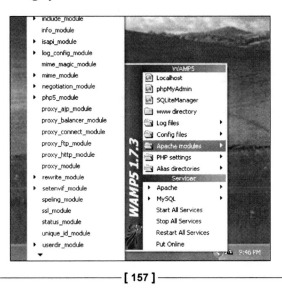

Versions of Apache, MySQL, and PHP for Windows are all available on the same websites mentioned above. As Windows doesn't have an apt-get kind of utility, you'll have to download and install all three components from their respective websites, but you have an easier way to set up a WAMP server. There are several pre-packaged Apache, MySQL, and PHP software bundles available for Windows (http://en.wikipedia.org/wiki/Comparison_of_WAMPs). I've successfully run Elgg on the WAMP5 bundle (http://www.en.wampserver.com/). The developer updates the bundle, time and again, to make sure it's running the latest versions of all server components included in the bundle.

> While WAMP5 requires no configuration, make sure you have Apache's `rewrite_module` and PHP's `php_gd2` extension enabled. They will have a bullet next to their name if they are enabled. If the bullet is missing, click on the respective entries under the Apache and PHP sub-categories and restart WAMP5.

Installing Elgg

Now that we have a platform ready for Elgg, let's move on to the most important step of setting up Elgg. Download the latest version of Elgg from its website. At the time of writing this book, the latest version of Elgg was Elgg-0.8. Elgg is distributed as a zipped file.

To uncompress under Linux: Move this zipped file to `/tmp` and uncompress it with the following command:

```
$ unzip /tmp/elgg-0.8.zip
```

To uncompress under Windows: Right-click on the ZIP file and select the **Extract here** option.

After uncompressing the ZIP file, you should have a directory called `elgg-<version-number>`, in my case, `elgg-0.8/`. This directory contains several sub-directories and files. The INSTALL file contains detailed installation instructions. The first step is to move this uncompressed directory to your web server.

> You can set up Elgg on your local web server that sits on the Internet or on a paid web server in a data center anywhere on the planet. The only difference between the two setups is that if you don't have access to the local web server, you'll have to contact the web service provider and ask him about the transfer options available to you. Most probably, you'll have FTP access to your web server, and you'll have to use one of the dozens of FTP clients, available for free, to transfer Elgg's files from your computer to the remote web server. Optionally, if you have "shell" access on the web server, you might want to save time by transferring just the zipped file and unzipping it on the web server itself. Contact your web server provider for this information.

The webserver's directory where you need to copy the contents of the Elgg directory depends upon your Apache installation and operating system. In Ubuntu Linux, the default web server directory is `/var/www/`. In Windows, WAMP5 asks where it should create this directory during installation. By default, it's the www directory and is created within the directory you installed WAMP5 under.

> Another important decision you need to make while installing Elgg is how do you want your users to access your network. If you're setting up the network to be part of your existing web infrastructure, you'll need to install Elgg inside a directory. If, on the other hand, you are setting up a new site just for the Elgg-powered social network, copy the contents of the Elgg directory inside the www directory itself and not within a sub-directory.

Once you have the Elgg directory within your web server's www directory, it's time to set things in motion. Start by renaming the `config-dist.php` file to `config.php` and the `htaccess-dist` to `.htaccess`. Simply right-click on the file and give it a new name or use the mv command in this format:

```
$ mv <original-file-name> <new-file-name>
```

> To rename `htacces-dist` to `.htaccess` in Windows, you'll have to open the `htaccess-dist` file in notepad and then go to **File | Save As** and specify the name as `.htaccess` with the quotes.

Editing config.php

Believe it or not, we've completed the "installation" bit of setting up Elgg. But we still need to configure it before throwing the doors open to visitors. Not surprisingly, all this involves is creating a database and editing the `config.php` file to our liking.

Creating a Database

Making an empty database in MySQL isn't difficult at all. Just enter the MySQL interactive shell using your username, password, and hostname you specified while installing MySQL.

```
$ mysql -u root -h localhost -p

Enter password:

Welcome to the MySQL monitor.  Commands end with ; or \g.

Your MySQL connection id is 9 to server version: 5.0.22-Debian_
0ubuntu6.06.3-log

Type 'help;' or '\h' for help. Type '\c' to clear the buffer.

mysql> CREATE DATABASE elgg;
```

You can also create a MySQL database using a graphical front-end manager like PHPMyAdmin, which comes with WAMP5. Just look for a database field, enter a new name (elgg), and hit the **Create** button to create an empty Elgg database.

Initial Configuration

Elgg has a front-end interface to set up config.php, but there are a couple of things you need to do before you can use that interface:

1. Create a data directory outside your web server root. As described in the configuration file, this is a special directory where uploaded files will go. It's also advisable to create this directory outside your main Elgg install. This is because this directory will be writable by everyone accessing the Elgg site and having such a "world-accessible" directory under your Elgg installation is a security risk.

   If you call the directory elgg-data, make it world-readable with the following command:

   ```
   $ chmod 777 elgg-data
   ```

2. Setup admin username and password. Before you can access Elgg's configuration web front-end, you need an admin user and a password. For that open the config.php file in your favorite text editor and scroll down to the following variables:

   ```
   $CFG->adminuser = "";
   $CFG->adminpassword = "";
   ```

Specify your chosen admin username and password between the quotes, so that it looks something like this:

```
$CFG->adminuser = "admin";
$CFG->adminpassword = "765thyr3";
```

Make sure you don't forget the username and password of the admin user.

Important Settings

When you have created the data directory and specified an admin username and password, it's time to go ahead with the rest of the configuration. Open a web browser and point to `http://<your-web-server>/<elgg-installation>/_elggadmin/`.

This will open up a simple web page with lots of fields. All fields have a title and a brief description of the kind of information you need to fill in that field. There are some drop-down lists as well, from which you have to select one of the listed options. Here are all the options and their descriptions:

Administration panel username: Username to log in to this admin panel, in future, to change your settings.

Admin password: Password to log in to this admin panel in future.

Site name: Enter the name of your site here (e.g. **Elgg, Apcala, University of Bogton's Social Network**, etc.).

Tagline: A tagline for your site (e.g. **Social network for Bogton**).

Web root: External URL to the site (e.g. **http://elgg.bogton.edu/**).

Elgg install root: Physical path to the files (e.g. **/home/elggserver/httpdocs/**).

Elgg data root: This is a special directory where uploaded files will go. If possible, this should live outside your main Elgg installation? (you'll need to create it by hand). It must have world writable permissions set, and have a final slash at the end.

> Even in Windows, where we use back slashes (\) to separate directories, use Unix's forward slashes (/) to specify the path to the install root, data root, and other path names. For example, if you have Elgg files under WAMP's default directory in your C drive, use this path: `C:/wamp/www/elgg/`.

Database type: Acceptable values are **mysql** and **postgres** - MySQL is highly recommended.

System administrator email: The email address your site will send emails from (e.g. **elgg-admin@bogton.edu**).

News account initial password: The initial password for the 'news' account. This will be the first administrator user within your system, and you should change the password immediately after the first time you log in.

Default locale: Country code to set language to if you have `gettext` installed.

Public registration: Can general members of the public register for this system?

Public invitations: Can users of this system invite other users?

Maximum users: The maximum number of users in your system. If you set this to 0, you will have an unlimited number of users.

Maximum disk space: The maximum disk space taken up by all uploaded files.

Disable public comments: Set the following to true to force users to log in before they can post comments, overriding the per-user option. This is a handy sledgehammer-to-crack-a-nut tactic to protect against comment spam (although an Akismet plug-in is available from elgg.org).

Email filter: Anything you enter here must be present in the email address of anyone who registers; e.g. @mycompany.com will only allow email address from mycompany.com to register.

Default access: The default access level for all new items in the system.

Disable user templates: If this is set, users can only choose from available templates rather than defining their own.

Persistent connections: Should Elgg use persistent database connections?

Debug: Set this to 2047 to get ADOdb error handling.

RSS posts maximum age: Number of days for which to keep incoming RSS feed entries before deleting them. Set this to 0 if you don't want RSS posts to be removed.

Community create flag: Set this to **admin** if you would like to restrict the ability to create communities to admin users.

cURL path: Set this to the cURL executable if cURL is installed; otherwise leave blank.

According to Wikipedia, cURL is a command line tool for transferring files with URL syntax, supporting FTP, FTPS, HTTP, HTTPS, TFTP, SCP, SFTP, Telnet, DICT, FILE, and LDAP. The main purpose and use for cURL is to automate unattended file transfers or sequences of operations. For example, it is a good tool for simulating a user's actions at a web browser.

Under Ubuntu Linux, you can install curl using the following command:

```
apt-get install curl
```

Templates location: The full path of your `Default_Template` directory.

Profile location: The full path to your profile configuration file (usually, it's best to leave this in `mod/profile/`).

Finally, when you're done, click on the **Save** button to save the settings.

The next version of Elgg, Elgg 0.9, will further simplify installation. Already an early release candidate of this version (elgg-0.9rc1) is a lot more straightforward to install and configure, for initial use.

First Log In

Now, it's time to let Elgg use these settings and set things up for you. Just point your browser to your main Elgg installation (`http://<your-web-server>/<elgg-installation>`). It'll connect to the MySQL database and create some tables, then upload some basic data, before taking you to the main page.

On the main page, you can use the news account and the password you specified for this account during configuration to log in to your Elgg installation.

Congratulations!

B
Elgg Case Study

All through the book, I've shown-off Elgg's malleability and how customizable it is to mold into your web infrastructure. But like the punch line in the Mobil 1 "Drive Around the World" expedition advertisement, "the real test is in the real world".

Elgg has been deployed to power all sorts of social networks around the world. From non-profits organizations in Colombia to sports fan communities, Elgg provides a platform for interaction to students in universities across continents, and a network to facilitate communication between educators interested in electronic learning.

Let's take a detailed look at some of the Elgg implementations.

Enabling Non-Profits in Colombia

So where does Elgg fit into a non-profits online presence? What hole does it plug? I discussed this with Diego Andrés Ramirez, Technology Director at Somos Más in Bogota, Colombia. Somos Más (meaning: We are more) is a Non Government Organization (NGO) that works towards the articulation of non-profits in Colombia.

Ramirez and his team have setup two networks based on Elgg—RedPai `http://redpai.org`, a network of child protection non-profits and RedReiri `http://redreiri.org`, a network of non-profits that work for people with physical disabilities.

Ramirez and his team saw the social networking platforms as a way to help the organizations get together, share important information between them, and more efficient interactions. With time being one of the scarcest and more important resources in non-profit organizations, the time the organizations spend in getting along and working with other organizations to solve more high-level problems (like articulation of the offer and demand of social services, public policy problems, qualification and pertinence of the service they are offering, and so on) is very valuable.

However, as per Ramirez, traditional methods of networking weren't efficient enough. Also, the organizations were spending a great deal of the time they had together in sharing basic information and resolving administrative problems. A dedicated social network is what was required to streamline the process of communication.

Before they found Elgg, the team had been developing their own GPL'ed system for building social networking sites. However, one day while looking for information about social networking on Wikipedia, they found Elgg, reviewed it, and found that it already had many of the features that they wanted. So, they decided to throw away their code and aligned their efforts with Elgg to build the social networking engine that would fit with their requirements.

According to Ramirez, their networks are unlike any other Elgg installation. Both their current setups include functionalities to allow non-profits to publish and promote their projects, services, and products as special types of content. Additionally, they have customized the graphic design and tweaked some features taking into account some usability considerations. For example, they had to let go many functionalities that come with Elgg for the sake of reducing the complexity for their target users who have little experience with this type of virtual social platform. You can probably understand this when you take into account some of Ramirez's statistics. Less than 10% of their current users know or have heard of what a blog is, and none of them have ever written a blog.

Like many developing countries, Internet connectivity is a big issue in Colombia. Ramirez and his team customized Elgg's page design to keep the download size of the pages very small, because a high number of the non-profits that use the system have a low bandwidth, or even a classic 56K telephone connection to the Internet.

But has the network helped? Not only are the organizations interacting with each other better, but Ramirez is all smiles when he says that for many of the non-profits present in their current installations, the platform his team has set up is the organization's only online presence. Some of them even refer people to their profile pages as their institutional page even though this wasn't the original idea.

So how has Ramirez's experience been working on Elgg? He says that from a developer's point of view, once you understand some of Elgg's idiosyncrasies it's an easy and powerful tool that you can use to build whatever you want. In his case, Elgg's two strongest points were that it allowed them to modify Elgg to fit their usability demands, and secondly, presented no difficulties adding new features that were useful for their clients—in record time and without too much effort.

In fact, some of the custom tools Ramirez and his team have developed have been released to the Elgg community as plug-ins. We've covered the most important and useful ones in the book. The plug-ins they have already released include:

- messages, `http://elgg.org/mod/plugins/plugin.php?id=18`: Private messages functionality

- siteusers, `http://elgg.org/mod/plugins/plugin.php?id=29`: Improvements over the `sitemembers` plug-in that'll show a wall of users as well as communities using custom templates.

- projects, `http://elgg.org/mod/plugins/plugin.php?id=41`: An extension over the `blog` plug-in that lets you manage projects.

- suggest, `http://elgg.org/mod/plugins/plugin.php?id=43`: An extension to the `similarusers` plug-in that suggests users and contents based in the **interests** field in the user profile.

- template_wrapper, `http://elgg.org/mod/plugins/plugin.php?id=28`: A system that lets you change the template used for displaying any specific page without the need to change any code.

There are several other plug-ins that they'll be launching soon including:

- **o2ohome**: Their custom profile home.
- **o2osidebar**: Their custom sidebar.
- **o2olists**: Their custom list for showing users and communities in an ordered way.
- **inlineposticon**: A blog extension that lets you add a custom profile for your post.
- **phplist**: Integration of phplist with Elgg.
- **polls**: A basic polls plug-in.

Ramirez offers some advice to non-profits contemplating on using a social networking platform like Elgg. From his experience in Colombia, he thinks there are mainly two serious obstacles that keep non-profits from taking more advantage of this type of platform and technologically-mediated solutions: sensibility and resources. And he thinks these two issues are related to each other because many non-profits don't think about the opportunities these solutions provide for them. They feel they can never get the resources to make interesting things happen.

However, Ramirez clarifies that this is more of a mental constraint than a real one. Operating a technologically obsolete non-profit is much more expensive than one that's more "technologically inclined". According to Ramirez, the cost involved in running a traditional "offline" setup (physical mail, national and international phone calls, papers, photocopies, and so on) are "just breathtaking".

Now, on the contrary, in many small and mid sized non-profits of between 25 to 50 people in staff, Ramirez found a quick return of investment when buying new hardware. Figuratively speaking, buying new "decent" computers for the administrative staff (lets say, 3 to 5 computers), and a "decent" Internet connection (that is to say they don't have to connect by traditional phone line by modem), the costs were recovered in 3 to 6 months.

Painting an all too familiar picture Ramirez mentions that some non-profits don't invest in technology because they feel that those resources would make them reduce their number of beneficiaries. Hence less resources equate to less means of providing services to beneficiaries. And also, in Colombia, the price of acquiring technology and decent Internet connections are some times higher than in other, more "connected" countries. Of course, Colombia isn't an isolated example. This is true of big countries and technology hubs like India and other South East Asian countries and even some European ones.

For Ramirez, getting non-profits hooked on to technology enablers like a social networking platform requires more than just telling and persuading. For him, it's a task of demo'ing—showing that not only the possibilities but also convincing them that it's well within their budgets. Ramirez is happy with the progress he and his team are making, and having piloted a couple of networks, it seems they're on the right track.

Connecting Campuses Spread Across the UK

The University of Brighton in England is split into several campuses many miles apart. The University's learning technologies group manager, Stan Stanier, stumbled upon Elgg while looking for a solution to get everyone (students and faculty) on the same page, literally.

Like many universities, Brighton too was using the standard virtual learning environment (VLE) facilities provided by Blackboard. Stanier describes these VLE's as "institutionally ring-fenced" due to their traditional model of learning and teaching. As per him, the VLE model, irrespective of what product you're using, is pretty much the same—tutor-led, students use it to download materials but there's very little room for student contributions. But adding Elgg to this mix, massively increased the range of facilities and possibilities for innovative learning and teaching.

Brighton's Elgg deployment, called Community@Brighton [`http://community.brighton.ac.uk/`], has more than 36,000 users—all staff and students get their own blog, file storage, and access to communities and other resources.

Stanier says that Elgg breaks many barriers including those between staff and students and between academic and social lives. As the university is split across several campuses, the student community has effectively been a bunch of separate smaller communities based around the campus. Elgg has now provided them with a real virtual platform to form a cohesive online student community across those geographical barriers.

Even more exciting for Stanier is the fact that Elgg provides a host of facilities for encouraging the formation of virtual communities and groups. These allow students to enjoy each-other's virtual company, learn together or support each other. They've seen a number of examples where students have blogged about feeling lonely, being stressed over course work or being unhappy with living-in student accommodation because of noise or feeling homesick, and so on. What has been really nice is that, through Elgg, the students have received lots of mutual support, offers of help and encouragement from other students as well as direct contact with relevant support services. Elgg has proved a very valuable tool in helping students resolve such problems.

From an educational point of view, Stanier believes that Elgg has a clear potential to provide Personal Learning Environments and ePortfolios, but it goes way beyond that and provides the platform for a shared learning environment—where all learners and teachers can contribute to their learning and the learning of others in the future.

Students can now contribute resources, ideas, and materials to virtual lessons/ discussions in exactly the same way tutors can, so Elgg offers far more of a parallel with a real-world seminar than a traditional VLE model, observes Stanier. Furthermore, he adds that because Elgg allows people to pull in RSS feeds and share them, as well as easily allowing external experts to participate, the community of learners and resources has widened beyond the institutional boundaries. Elgg allows learners shared access to a much wider range of knowledge and opinion than a traditional VLE system.

The University of Brighton was one of the early users of Elgg. Stanier agrees it was a risk deploying a product so early in its development stage but it allowed them to work with the Elgg developers and shape the development of Elgg to meet the needs of such a wide-scale institutional implementation. Some of these "demands" included automated user registrations, memberships, and account creation using the same data feeds we use for our VLE (blackboard), LDAP authentication, and additional default settings to meet the needs of our staff and students.

Before finalizing on Elgg, the university tried several other collaborations systems `http://asymptomatic.net/blogbreakdown.htm`. But from a technical perspective, they had some very specific needs in order to be able to roll out the service to the whole institution. And none of the systems listed, satisfied all those requirements at the time. Also, when he was out looking Stanier contacted many developers and user-communities of other social technologies but had very few positive or helpful responses. The Elgg developers, on the other hand, couldn't have been more approachable or helpful says Stanier adding that he was impressed by the commitment, dedication, and vision of its developers.

From a technical side, Stanier notes that Elgg is extremely easy to customize, write plug-ins for, integrates into other technologies, provides a wide variety of facilities, and is constantly being developed and improved. Jokingly, he adds that the only drawback they've identified is not fully implementing all the ideas that spring to mind about how they could use it creatively!

Other Elgg Networks

In addition to these are a couple of other Elgg networks I'd like to point out:

- Elgg.org [`http://www.egg.org/`] – A community of Elgg developers and users, maintained by the developers of Elgg. Although this site runs Elgg, the developers have completely removed some menu options, and hidden other features. The index page has been revamped, and they wrote a new custom plug-in to house links to other plug-ins. As per the developers, this site taught them a number of interesting lessons about supporting an open source software platform.

- Rucku [`http://www.rucku.com/`] – First social network on Rugby. Built by the Elgg developers for TotalEdge Networks. The underlying software is Elgg 0.8, with a number of plug-ins added over the top and some other tinkering; much like elgg.org, they've removed some features and added others.

- Swatch the Club [`http://www.swatchtheclub.com/`] – Online community of Swatch customers. It's a heavily customized Elgg installation.

- Ubuntero [http://ubuntero.org/] – An upcoming community of Ubuntu users and developers. They have interesting communities including those for game development, packaging, and virtual regional communities.

Summary

As we've seen throughout this book, Elgg is a very diverse platform for opening up lines of communication where none exist. In this chapter, we've seen examples of Elgg deployments in very different continents to serve very different purposes.

Elgg's customizability is unique. Not only is it designed to add on new features, but as in the case of non-profits in Colombia, it can scale down its features as well. You can gauge its flexibility from the fact that its deployers in Colombia were able to iron it out for non-technical users — users who had never even blogged before!

Another aspect of Elgg, highlighted by its use in Colombian non-profits and underlined by its implementers in the university in UK, is the strength of its community. Like a true Open Source product, Elgg is developed for the community, by the community. Some of its very important plug-ins have been contributed by its users.

Elgg's third biggest strength, as appreciated by its use in the university, is its ability to co-exist with existing web infrastructure. Be it VLE's in an educational institute or Wiki's and Forums on the intranet or world facing websites, Elgg can fit nicely with the most popular ones.

The main aim of this chapter has been to demonstrate that Elgg can be used in any situation, by the people who've used it themselves. No matter what your constraints or how challenging your objective, Elgg's capable enough to handle it all.

Index

Symbols

<div> tag 116
<span> tag 116

A

administration options
  about 46
  multiple users, adding 46, 47
  users, managing 47, 48
  user settings, changing 47, 48

B

blogs
  about 9, 61
  downloading 76, 77
  draft post plugin 66
  draft post plugin, downloading 67
  drafts, saving 65
  entry, posting 61, 62
  files, embedding 64, 65
  flagged posts, managing 70
  friends blog link 68
  improper posts, flagging 69, 70
  improper posts, handling 69
  posts, deleting 68
  posts, editing 67
  posts, filtering 71
  posts, marking as private 65, 66
  private post, disadvantages 66
  unique number 65
  video, adding 62-64

C

Captcha plugin 72
community
  about 10
  administration 97
  blog 96
  blog, viewing 96
  content viewing, community blog 96
  creating 87
  deleting 97
  existing, searching for 88
  forum 99-101
  grooming 89
  improper posts, removing 97
  joining 92
  leaving 94
  membership requests, handling 93, 94
  membership restriction 93
  moderation levels, membership
    restriction 93
  new community, creating 88, 89
  ownership 95
  picture 90
  picture, uploading 90, 91
  profile 89
  profile, editing 89, 90
  searching for 88
  users, inviting 91
  using 95
community administration
  about 97
  file quota, changing 99
  WYSIWYG editor 99

Thank you for buying
Elgg Social Networking

Packt Open Source Project Royalties

When we sell a book written on an Open Source project, we pay a royalty directly to that project. Therefore by purchasing Elgg Social Networking, Packt will have given some of the money received to the Elgg Project.

In the long term, we see ourselves and you—customers and readers of our books—as part of the Open Source ecosystem, providing sustainable revenue for the projects we publish on. Our aim at Packt is to establish publishing royalties as an essential part of the service and support a business model that sustains Open Source.

If you're working with an Open Source project that you would like us to publish on, and subsequently pay royalties to, please get in touch with us.

Writing for Packt

We welcome all inquiries from people who are interested in authoring. Book proposals should be sent to authors@packtpub.com. If your book idea is still at an early stage and you would like to discuss it first before writing a formal book proposal, contact us; one of our commissioning editors will get in touch with you.

We're not just looking for published authors; if you have strong technical skills but no writing experience, our experienced editors can help you develop a writing career, or simply get some additional reward for your expertise.

About Packt Publishing

Packt, pronounced 'packed', published its first book "Mastering phpMyAdmin for Effective MySQL Management" in April 2004 and subsequently continued to specialize in publishing highly focused books on specific technologies and solutions.

Our books and publications share the experiences of your fellow IT professionals in adapting and customizing today's systems, applications, and frameworks. Our solution-based books give you the knowledge and power to customize the software and technologies you're using to get the job done. Packt books are more specific and less general than the IT books you have seen in the past. Our unique business model allows us to bring you more focused information, giving you more of what you need to know, and less of what you don't.

Packt is a modern, yet unique publishing company, which focuses on producing quality, cutting-edge books for communities of developers, administrators, and newbies alike. For more information, please visit our website: www.PacktPub.com.

WordPress Complete

ISBN: 1-904811-89-2   Paperback: 272 pages

A complete guide to successful learning using Moodle

1. Straight-forward coverage of installing and using the Moodle system

2. Working with Moodle features in all learning environments

3. A unique course-based approach focuses your attention on designing well structured, interactive, and successful courses

Building powerful and robust websites with Drupal 6

ISBN: 978-1-847192-97-4   Paperback: 330 pages

Build your own professional blog, forum, portal or community website with Drupal 6

1. Set up, configure, and deploy Drupal 6

2. Harness Drupal's world-class Content Management System

3. Design and implement your website's look and feel

4. Easily add exciting and powerful features

5. Promote, manage, and maintain your live website

Please check **www.PacktPub.com** for information on our titles

Printed in the United States
114310LV00002B/26/P

9 781847 192806